ASANTE SANA, 'THANK YOU'
FATHER JAMES E. GROPPI

Asante Sana, 'Thank You' Father James E. Groppi

Shirley R. (Berry) Butler-Derge, Ph.D.

Order this book online at www.trafford.com
or email orders@trafford.com

Most Trafford titles are also available at major online book retailers.

0-9717545-3-5 FIRST EDITION

Cover design courtesy of Wisconsin Historical Society Museum #ID 5295 1968
Cover Photograph, Father James Groppi singing with Milwaukee NAACP Youth Council
Members on the steps of St. Boniface Church in 1968. From the Milwaukee Journal Sentinel,
Journal Sentinel Inc., reproduced with permission, Wisconsin Historical Society #ID 5295.

Author's photograph by Fayemi D. Jackson
Library of Congress Cataloging-in-Publication Data

Dr. Shirley (Berry) Butler-Derge

Printed in the United States of America.

ISBN: 978-1-4269-4872-5 (sc)
ISBN: 978-1-4269-4874-9 (e)
ISBN: 978-1-4269-4873-2 (hc)

Library of Congress Control Number: 2010941116

Trafford rev. 10/24/2012

www.trafford.com
North America & international
toll-free: 1 888 232 4444 (USA & Canada)
phone: 250 383 6864 ♦ fax: 812 355 4082

DEDICATION

This book is dedicated to the following Milwaukee NAACP Youth Council Members, Commandos and other angels who participated in the Civil Rights/ Open Housing marches during the 1960's.

Attorney Lloyd A. Barbee
Vada Bass
James Beckley
Raymond Bladders
Carol Carmen Butler
Columbus Boston
Dennis Boyd
Kenneth Bowen
Cleavlin Bryant
Cecil Brown Jr.
Elizabeth Campbell
Rev. Leo Champion
Odean Childs
William Coffey
Brenda M. Coggs
Rose Marie Coggs
Isaac Coggs
Marsha Coggs
Velma L. Coggs
Thurston Coleman

Allen Crawford
Lawrence Friend
Marion "Red" Glass
Lawrence Gantt
Father James E. Groppi
Merlyn Morehouse Hansen
Webster Harris
LaVada Harris
Charles Harper
Ester Hazelwood
James Hazelwood
Joe Hazelwood
Joe Holloman
Edward Jamerson
Cheryl Jean-Jeter Johnson
Earl Johnson
Walter Jones
Jimmy Johnson
Rev. Albert Kelly Sr.
Sullivan King
Rev. Richard Kirkendoll
Hilda Larkey
Rev. R.L. Lathan
Milton Lanzing
Earl Lewis
Carol Thomas-Malone
Lee McGee Jr.
Lee McGee Sr.
Eugene Pierce
James Pierce
Donald Reed
David Rodgers
Ida Mae Royalty
Addie Mae Sargent
Rev. Lamont Sherman
Dalow Stingley

Robert Stingley
Clarence Smith
Claretta Simpson
Ivory Thornton
Ruby Toon
Duwayne Toliver
William Turner
AC Turner
Jessie Wade
John Ware
Carol Willis
Early Wilson
Cynthia Wigley
Bettie Lou Woods
Tommy Lee Woods
Sylvester Williams
Howard Wright
Estelle Yarbrough
Lucile Woodards

Special Thank you Honorable Vel R. Phillips

Compiled and read at the 40th Celebration of the Milwaukee NAACP Youth Council- March-On-Milwaukee (MOM) at the 16th street Bridge on September 29 2007.

By Fred Reed, Commando

ACKNOWLEDGEMENTS

Minnie Butler-McClain, my mother who taught me to *Never* bow my head in_shame for being an African Native American female. K.C. Butler, my father who was unable to march due to his "bad feet" but always made the best coffee and tea for the marchers. Father James E. Groppi, "Grop", adviser and founder of the Milwaukee NAACP Youth Council, who told me that my black skin, nappy hair, and wide thick lips were physical gifts from God. Professor Margaret "Peggy," widow of famous Father James E. Groppi, thanks for writing my first recommendation for Upward Bound at the University of Wisconsin-Milwaukee, including me in your play, *March on Milwaukee* and for being an outstanding role model. Carole Carmen Butler, my sister, who held my hand when we were lost at the age of five and for encouraging me to write, Mary Childs-Arms, my best friend who was arrested with me on the 100th day for fair/open housing protest march, Lee Mc Ghee Jr. for being my "big brother" at St. Boniface grade school and helping me create "freedom songs" during the marches, Tommy Lee Woods, "Red Glass," Duwayne Tollvier, Lawrence Friend and my sweet heart, Dennis Boyd, thanks for protecting me during the "Poor People Campaign" at Washington D.C., Aunt Elizabeth Campbell, Ida Mae Royalty, Mother Miller, and Estelle Yarbrough, thanks for your watchful eyes, motherly wisdom and all the bologna and cheese sandwiches after the marches. Sullivan & Jean Williams, thanks for the comfort of your car after a long cold march in the freezing rain, scorching heat and unbearable winter walks. Finally, Annie Evers, Charlene Evers, Fred Evers, Helen Evers, Lawrence Butler, Glenda Butler, Barbara Butler, Betty Martin-Harris, Vada Harris, Barbara & Jenny Davis, Pamela Sergeant, Angie Gray-Ward, The Harris sisters- Roberta, Claudetta, Lou-Lou and Wanda, Jimmy Harris, and Kenneth and Joyce McGhee, thank you all for uplifting our motto, "neither snow nor rain nor heat or gloom of the justice path stopped us from marching for a just cause."

INTRODUCTION

Forty years ago, thousands of Milwaukee residents marched for
equal rights to join and participate in local organizations, receive
equal and appropriate educational resources for their children, and
live where they wanted. Thus, the purpose of the book, **Asante
Sana, 'Thank You' Father James Groppi** is to commemorate and
honor Father James E. Groppi and the Milwaukee NAACP Youth
Council/Commandos who unselfishly put their lives on line and
made a significant difference in making Milwaukee's history one
that changed the livelihood for all living beings.

Specifically, in the book: Asante Sana, 'Thank You' Father
James Groppi, the author, who was one of the original founders
of the Milwaukee NAACP Youth Council in 1964, poetically
responds to some of the famous quotes of Father Groppi and the
Milwaukee NAACP Youth Council members while they encountered
challenging issues with racial discrimination (i.e., St. Boniface
Church/School: Marching/Rallies, Integration/Segregation, Eagles'
Club, Integration/Segregation in the Milwaukee Public Schools,
Milwaukee United School Integration Committee (MUSIC),
Segregation of Milwaukee Public Schools, Honorable Vel Phillips,
Dick Gregory, Freedom Schools, Freedom House, Washington
D.C. "Poor People Campaign," Black Christmas, Kosciusko Park,

Open Housing Marching, 16th Street Viaduct) and hate letters and/or comments received during the 1960's in Milwaukee.

From this book, the author wishes that all people celebrate their similarities and respect their differences as a human race.

CONTENTS

Father Groppi wearing black glasses marching with Milwaukee NAACP Junior Youth Council Members (*left* – Debra Campbell, *front center* – Glenda Butler, author's baby sister)

From the Milwaukee Journal Sentinel, Journal Sentinel Inc., reproduced with permission, Milwaukee Journal 1968.

My Little Sister: Glenda Butler

85 pounds, 5" 2 inches with dark huge wide eyes
Glenda knew, as she marched with her best friend, Debra Campbell
Around the six to twelve blocks
That stoned the ancient
Roman Catholic Elementary School
St. Boniface:

Dressed with armed body and mind
Focused on the purpose
To stand
To speak
"I am a human being with human rights"

Even at the age of 12
Milwaukee Junior NAACP Youth Council Members
Knew and ACCEPTED
Responsibility of the role:
No Time for jumping rope
No Time for playing Jacks
Nor
Bobbie Dolls
Instead: What do they do….
Jail if need be!

They shout out loud,
"What do you what?"
Freedom Now!"

"We have the right to live where we want!"
No
"One has the right to say where I should go to school"
Even at the young age of 12
Glenda was prepared
Umbrella in hand for the familiar hail storm
Prepared to die
Glenda knew as she marched with pride
Without fear
Veiled with Father Groppi's protected heart
Glenda marched with best friend, Debra Campbell

Milwaukee United Schools Integrated Congregation (MUSIC) activists engaged in civil disobedience, blocking intact busing at the peak of their movement in 1965.
(left to right Marylyn Morehouse, Minnie Butler, author's mother, 'Muddear' and Attorney Lloyd Barbee).

From the *Milwaukee Journal*, May 24, 1965; copyright Milwaukee Journal Sentinel, Inc.; reproduced with permission.

My Muddear: Making M.U.S.I.C.

My Muddear frowned on a musical hate:
Racism
Discrimination
Segregation

My Muddear's frown
Made her eye brows
Join to make a star on her angry wise forehead
That warned others:
YOU BETTER WATCH OUT!

That's the look My Muddear says she would wear on her face
With her black thick brim eyeglasses
That sees through all wrongs
The night before she chained herself
To the segregated bus at the McDowell school site

Other freedom fighters stood by like watchful eagles
Father Groppi
Attorney Lloyd Barbee
As guardian angels energized their foot steps

My Muddear questioned:
"Why they closing down inner city schools
And busing our black babies away across town?"

"...two hours going and two hours coming back.
Lawd knows something ain't right with that!"

My Muddear says,
"When the Black babies gets to the White schools
They still all put in the same room
With the same Black teachers

Our Black babies even eat in separate rooms from the White
children
And
They call that
INTEGEGATION!

My Muddear says,
"This here
McDowell School site they be building
Is not for our neighborhood

"Specialty Schools"
That's what they call them
In other words
'Maybe 1-2 Black children will be allowed.

My Muddear says,
"Over my dead body
I will stand up for myself and my children
Chain myself to this here old segregated school bus.
I ain't goin' to let nobody turn me around!"

Father Groppi: My Journey

At the tender age of 15
i discovered that Black people were
Stolen
Beaten
Raped
Murdered and forced into stinky ships
Sold in America,
And other parts of the world.

RESULT:
i vowed to never wear anything white
Shoes
Skirts
Shirts
i decided along with my best friend,
Lee McGhee Jr., Vice-President of the NAACP Youth Council/
Commando
To detest all white people

7 days we did not engage in a conversation
With that white priest Father Groppi

However, with the grace of love
From
A white priest with a smile that melted and
Open hearts
Healing pain prior to its purpose
Seeing rose bud thoughts
Like diamonds in the rough
That blossomed with endearment
Hope
Purpose
No More shame

"Your kinky, black hair is so beautiful"
Did you know that your smooth black skin has healing properties
of its own?

Direction
So, as you grow, you will learn the real truth
About Black people
Just promise yourself, that you see and treasure your precious inner
gifts
Share them with those that need uplifting
Just Remember as you travel on your journey
Don't join the hater
Be the change maker

Police: Watching Little Me

Sweetly humming my favorite freedom song
"This little light of mine,
I am goin' to let it shine"
Only four blocks to my brown and white house on
1526 West Burleigh Street

I noticed from the left corner of my shoulder
A medium size white car with
Two huge white policemen slowly
But surely cruising by
As my fifteen year old little self shivered with fear.

The summer's heat unveiled past warnings,
"When you see them –
Don't Stop! Don't Run!
Just Keep on Steppin'
As if you Don't See THEM!"
FBI that's their name if they aren't dressed in blue or black with a
huge
Black stick they call a club

Were the soothing, wise words of Father Groppi
Sweetly gave at the NAACP Youth Council meeting just a week ago

Man, I was so relieved to turn the corner on 15th Burleigh Street
And see my Muddear standing on our white and brown
Porch on a hill waving her hand in the air
"Shelley, Shelley" she shouted, Why are you so late?

"Muddear! Muddear!" I urgently responded.
Waving back, Muddear nervously said, "Child, you should have
been home
Awhile ago
Your NAACP Youth Council meeting was over 2 hours.
What took you so long?"

Feeling the hunger to express my delay
I made my feet jump ahead two hot beats while I explained
As I skipped forward crossing the street,

I went to the rectory with the rest of the group
To eat some homemade Italian sausages
From Father Groppi's family store
Before you know – two hours had passed."

Eagerly embracing my Muddear on the porch
Fear buried itself
As the heavenly smell of cinnamon and nutmeg waltzed across my
nose
From the sweet potato pies into kitchen oven

2 minutes passed peeking through the living curtains
Short living serenity
Teen heart beating like a Dejembe drum
I panicked and scream
"Muddear, Muddear!
Those same two white cops that followed me home
From St. Boniface
They still outside
Parked outside in front of our house!
They are talking on their hand radios!"

Taking off her apron and laying it on the kitchen chair
Quickly slipping off house shoes
Making a frown on her face that said

Yall all Better Watch Out Now!
I am the storm
Something is definitely wrong
With this here picture

Muddear announced with anger,
"Well, child, we will see about that right
Now!"

Gliding down eight flights of stairs
In one short breath
With her right hand on her hip
Muddear quickly instructed,
"You come on and stand beside me."

Marching straight up to the police in the car
Muddear questioned with a mother's alarm,
"Are you all the police?"
"I asked you a question. Are you the police?"

"Madam, you are obstructing traffic, please vacant the premise"
Coldly, one police responded without looking at Muddear or me.

With the frown still on her face, Muddear demanded body
expression
Hand remaining on her right hip
Not blinking an eye, Muddear repeated with a mother's raged,

"I will ask you one more time, are you the police?"

"Madam, you are obstructing traffic, please vacant the premise"
Without turning his head in our direction the second policemen
Repeated the first policemen,
"Madam, you are obstructing traffic, please vacant the premise"

Like the Commandos on guard at every march
My Muddear fearlessly stated,
"Oh, you all are *not* the police."
Then answer this, Do you all live in the neighborhood?"

As if they were deaf, the police continued to chant,
"Madam, you are obstructing traffic, please vacant the premise"

Remaining as cool as a tack,
Muddear asked one more time with a firm voice,
"If you are NOT the police
And you DON"T live in the neighborhood,
Then tell me just one thing,
"Why are you two grown white men sitting in?
Front of *MY House*
Watching *MY Daughters?*"

Responding like lifeless robots the police continued to say
"Madam, you are obstructing traffic, please vacant the premise"

Fed-up with the policemen's lack of reluctance
Muddear sternly announced
Still with her hand on her hip,
Oh …Okay, I got yall number.
I am going to call the police."

Swiftly turning as though Muddear controlled
All seasons of the Mother Nature
Muddear stormed into the house
And called the *police* on the *police*

"There is a white car parked in front of
MY House with two *grown white men.*"
'They sitting in front of *My House*
Watching *my daughters!*"
"They *Don't* live in the neighborhood
And
"They actin' "*real*" crazy!"
You all better send somebody out here real quick
Before I am tempered to go back out here
And use my *Big* thick black stick!"

Commandos: The Name

Mid July 1960
Sitting down on the middle
Of the cold hard wooden floor
At our 3rd street office building,

Mary Ann Childs, NAACP Youth Council member and I
Were drawing posters:
Freedom Now!
Equal Rights for ALL!
Fair Housing!
Integrated Schools!

Mary Ann thoughtfully said,
"We need men to protect us
From those "Crazy" folks
When we are marching!"

"We should call them
COMMANDOS!"

As we are marching outside in
Rain
Snow and those
Chilly evenings

COMMANDOS
Guard the marchers
Standing tall with their NAACP Youth Council T-shirts
Outside the marchers' line
Eagle eyes sometimes
Accompanied with trained fist

Courageous Bold eagles began
Guarding angels as we continued to march with
A fierce thirst for
Justice.

Eagle's Club: Patty Wagon

Coming around the corner on 24th Wisconsin Avenue
Altar Boys at the tender age of 18
Lawrence Butler
Lee McGhee Jr. and Kenney McGhee
Were arrested at the Eagle's Club

No black people were allowed
To be members
Yet
Two white judges from Milwaukee
Were embraced by the founder brothers

What's wrong with this picture?
Challenging youthful hearts
Began to harp!
Amidst, crushing young dreams

Dragged on the early winter
Freezing concert ground
7 feet
250 pounds
White cops hosted my brother 120
Pounds in mid air
Throwing him into an open dark door

Clawing my way through the circle of police
I screamed, "Lawie, Lawie"

Over my shoulder, I heard a
Male uncompromising voice,

"You let him go!"
Leaping in the sky
Over my shoulders like "superman"
Lee McGhee Jr.
Shouted, "Man, you don't need to kick me in my ribs.
Man, Okay, Okay, I am stepping into the patty wagon

This scene was like watching the senseless
Plot in Mississippi when the cops
Charged trained killer "Nigger" dogs
On helpless protestors who refused to
Leave the "white only" restaurant.

Bang!
The doors to the patty wagon shut tight!

Standing paralyzed
Speechless
Beckoned by a much higher
Power to witness
My brother Lawrence, Lee and Kenny McGhee
Faces glowed with timeless pride
Through the dusty pale windows of the patty wagon
Drove by
As my trembling knees welcomed the
Comforting sounds of the maple trees
Wind message,
"Stick to the plan.
Daddy will get them out."

Spirit finding strength, as it song its favorite tune through hot
Streaming tears
"I Ain't Goin' Let NOBODY Turn Me Around!"

Groppi Protesting Eagle's Club, 1966

Father Groppi and the Milwaukee NAACP Youth Council members demonstrating outside on a chilly night at the Eagles' Club, a "White Only" club. Blacks were allowed to "perform" but not "join."

Wisconsin Historical Society WHi-53595

Aunt Elizabeth:
St. Boniface Cook

Aunt Elizabeth, Aunt Elizabeth
Smiling wide spreading
Love
Filling you up with
Warm maple brown buttered pancakes.

Stirring huge iron kettles and pots
With comfort, advice
Cooking-up Sunday morn with
Hot juicy Jimmy Dean Sausages
Crispy fried bacon so sweetly lay to the side with
Fluffy scrambled eggs

However, never missing a side stir of advice
From an elder who had lived a long life,

"You girls better get some education and
Put them young boys last on your list."
Get hungry and get as many degrees as you can!"
Aunt Elizabeth announced as she lifted a pan of grits
That sat on top of the church stove.
"Hummmm, store up that knowledge for them rainy days ahead.
Cause you never know what's coming around the corner."
She continued to warn.

Thin bologna and cheese sandwiches
Lovingly wrapped between white Wonder Bread
Enthusiastically washed down with cold milk
200 endless chilly nights

Awaited dinners served for us marchers.
Forever delivered with a jubilant chuckle.
Yeah, that was Aunt Elizabeth.

An irresistible Mother to all in need
Bread for strength
Sweet Rolls, for comfort
Given away freely to an extended hand

Aunt Elizabeth's warmhearted tenderness
Filled the hearts of loads of.
Marchers
Assuring them confidence just as tight as the apron she
Daily worn
Securely wrapped around her
Curvy hips
As Aunt Elizabeth generously served up
Love, comfort and advice
Even for
Father Groppi:

"Me and the other mothers-
Muddear
Momma Miller
Mrs. Royalty and Mrs. McGhee
Says, you better keep them Commandos away from our girls"

"...and if I sees any of them messing with our girls,
Muddear will whip them with her boots
And I am going after them with this here
Big Sliver Dipping Spoon"

Yeah, Aunt Elizabeth could surely stir up some tasteful yolk
And she let people know she was nobody's joke!

Center female, **Aunt Elizabeth, cook at St. Boniface School and during the open-housing marches.** *Back left female*, **Barbara Butler, author's sister.** *Right female*, **Shirley Butler-Derge, author in St. Boniface's kitchen with two other NACCP Youth Council Commandos in 1967.**

Photo by Fred Reed, Commando.

WANTED:
Have You Seen this Man?

Description:
Goes by the Name of: Father Groppi
Sometimes: "Grup"
Gender: Male
Race: White
Wardrobe: Black shirt & pants w/white collar:

Five feet, six inches
160 pounds
Thick short curly black hair
White male priest
Oval black trim glasses
Medium size dark brown eyes

Wanted:
- Loving all his sisters and brothers regardless of what color
- Shouting out loud the injustices that occurred: Milwaukee, Wisconsin
- Refusing to feed himself while his neighbors were hungry, homeless, and jobless
- Telling the Mayor that he should use the city's funding for
- Unemployed
- Fair-Housing
- Not for a beautiful fountain in front of the city hall
- Telling black children that they are made in God's image,
- Thus nappy hair, big thick lips and a flat wide nose is a
- Divine gifts from the Creator!
- Gathering whites and blacks together to protest against:
    Discrimination
    Segregation
    Most of all, claiming he was a man of God
                And
    He DID what his Father told him to DO!
    LOVE EVERYBODY!!

Father James E. Groppi
[He Touched Lives of a Generation]
"You will always be my Father!" **Astante Sana, 'Thank You'**
Father James Groppi.
Dr. Shirley R. (Berry) Butler-Derge
2010

Barbara Davis – Salas
Father Groppi was a Great Religious Leader

"Father Groppi was what a religious leader is supposed to be. What religious leaders to be but aren't. He was passionate about the *church*. He taught the church it exists to serve people. St. Boniface's building was used to make a difference. Its pulpit used to teach as all religions should do – how to make the world a just place for *all* people. Not just Catholic, Jews, Muslims and other religions. He taught me that richness exists in the variety of people who we love who become a part of us."

Gathering of the Bread

Almost every Saturday evening
About 6:00 PM
Just before sunset
At least 40 eager young hearts
Beaming with hope
Lined around St. Boniface Overflowing with courage
Determined to walk through hell
Each young soul drank from the chalice
Swallowing their destiny to firmly stand
Forcing the wrong to note the time for CHANGE

Harmonizing their voices to one footstep
The life coil
The deliverance of a new birth:

One Spirit
One Nation
One People…The Human Race church's:
Golden bass altar
Wrapped warmed from the circle of.
Friendship

The ceiling clapped and praised
Curley's (commando) tenor melody that filled
The veins of young eagles
Smelling the sweet scent of transformation.

Father Groppi Gives Host at Mass

Center, **Father Groppi gives Mass on the
Altar at St. Boniface Church.
Two Milwaukee NAACP Youth Council Commandos
stand in attendance in 1967.**

From the *Milwaukee Journal*, October 1967; copyright Milwaukee
Journal Sentinel, Inc.; reproduced with permission.

Let the Church Say, AMEN!

St. Boniface's Mass housed over 2,000 on
Monday through Sunday during the 1960's

Every color under the rainbow
Arriving from the
North-side
South-side
East-side
And the West-side

With one goal,
Making a jubilant resonance of
Praise
Courage
Hope
A pledge to the universe for
Justice

As angelic voices of NAACP Youth Council members:
Shirley Butler
Pam Sergeant
"Curley"
Fred Reed
Wilma Arms
Betty Harris
Barbara Davis

Mary Ann & "Nippy" Childs
Joyce Wigley & Kenneth McGhee
Barbara, Carol, and Glenda Butler
Lee McGhee Jr.
Sheila & Gale Ray

Bounding off the ceiling
Musical marching freedom versus:

"We Shall Not, We Shall Not
We Shall Not, We Shall Not be Moved
Just like a tree planted by the water.
We Shall Not be Moved."

Hands clapping, Feet Stomping
Steadfast, youthful souls vowed
To fight for their human rights
As the audience echoed
AMEN!
As black angels jazzed on the altar
Blending
With the African Dejembe drums
Twirling and soaring
In circles to Psalm 23

As Father Groppi hosted the gleaming golden chalice
Faithfully announcing,

"Oh heavenly Father, protect us as we walk through
The valley of death -
Southside of Milwaukee today.
…continue to give us the strength the stand up against
Those that wish to destroy
The "equal rights" of all mankind

Heavenly Father, open up the
Closed hearts of our brothers and sisters who
Refuses to acknowledge that All people,
Jews,
Catholics,

Protestants
Muslims
Or
Atheisms
Are human beings
And that let this day become the day:
A New Day of Breaking into a new arisen
Seeds for the Nile
Crops for the unborn
Let's like the church say.
AMEN!

Groppi Moralistic, Not Political
He wanted to expose wrongs.
He was not concerned about political ramifications.

"Grup" The Change Maker

Some people choose to go through life
By just looking at the scenery
And adding an occasional plastic flower
Every now and then
NOT
Grup!
Wherever fear dared to peep its ugly tail in someone's
Dreams
To destroy the soul
The spirit of the people

Grup!
Took center stage:
Education:
Down with *Segregation*
Challenging the narrow path for fair hiring
Shaking up the selfish consciousness

Allen Bradley:
Demanding an end to the old
Persistent rule that black men
Lack the" thinking skills"
To acquire the lesson to identify the purpose
Of a working tool

Fair-housing
Gathering the ancestral warriors
To demolish those that harvest
Seeds only for the "master's"
Plantation

Forcing the Eagle's Club to
Polish its Bronze doors
So that they may view the reflections
Of its gifted black, red and yellow
Brothers and sisters too!

Grup chose to listen to the beat pulsate of the Nile River, his heart.
Thus, he realized his being was just a small ripple of the Nile's
being.

Groppi Often Maudlin and Depressed

He worried about "not being accepted" or "not getting anywhere with what he was doing.

Human Angels

Do human angels exist here on earth?
While they are here
Are they *charged* to?
Wrap their ray of light-shadows
To catch and cover
The tears of others
Overwhelming need to
Blanket those who have no haven.

To empty the baggage
They are forced to carry
From shoulder to shoulder

Dreading to fill the desire to feed one's thirst
While brick cold alley concrete
Embraces the bellies of staving child

Yes
Only a human angel's
Throbbing heart splits and bleeds
The grief and anguish
His neighbors are forced to trail
The crooked ancient tears chained from the door of no return.

Black Leaders

Yes. That's right!
80 percent of the freedom fighters in
Milwaukee, Wisconsin in the 1960's
Rose up, gathered together

Children
Adults
Young
Old

Heard the cracking of thunder
Reverberating from the belly of mother earth
Echoing
Voices demanding equal share of the rivers that joins
And respects the people of the free lands

Organized
Black people form Sit-ins
In Mayor Henry Maier office
Picketed two-faced judges'
Manicured white fenced homes
With respectful signs:

**How Can you Live In a
Home with Heat
When Your Neighbor
Is Forced to Sleep in the Street?**

Marching over 300 miles
To set right the inhumane conditions Black
People were forced to endure.

No heat in the freezing winter months
Causing families of four or more
To build a campfire
From the wooden panels from the floor

Roaches luring their cousins from outside on the porch
To enter their cozy free rent homes

While newborns are too often found
Screaming in the middle of the night
Cause a rodent has bitten their little toes.

Yes, *That's* rights
Black leaders rose to the
Hollow muffled of their
Neighbor's meaningless plight
Shouting this dismay
MUST end today

Black leaders made the call to the universe
Standing by their decisions to fight this infective disease
Created from another's zest
To *steal* the *best*!

Atlas, joining hands
Latino, Native Americans, Asians, and whites
Supported this righteous human cause

Insults Hurled At Groppi Along the March
"Why don't you go to confession?"
"You nigger bastard."

NIGGER LOVER

Earsplitting ranting and raving crazed
"White Power" males
Standing on tops of "Bill's Used"1960 cars lot
With white T-shirts charcoal:
"NIGGER LOVER"
Lips twisted with annoyance
Revulsion

Madness governing their voices as they screamed
Uncontrollable chants:

"YOU, NIGGER LOVER
YOU, NIGGER BASTARDS"

As the marchers, Mary, Betty, Barbara, Nippy and Lee
Clutched hands and our teen bodies
Closed the gap between our narrowed focused footsteps

Singing in the mist of flying
Broken dreams
Glass, stones, bottles and the smell of
Human spit sputtered down one's cheek.

"I AIN'T GOIN' LET NOBODY TURN ME AROUND.
TURN ME AROUND
TURN ME AROUND
I AIN'T GOIN' TO LET NOBODY TURN ME AROUND."

Two arms length marching in between
Two Commandos
Father Groppi's right hand dabbed
Dripping red blood from the right-side of his temple
Immediately, after a coke bottle soared from
The "White Power" male group standing on "Bill's Used" car lot

Striking with intense force and bouncing off the side of
Father Groppi's blood stains face.
Hastening to his rescue
Dwight Benning and Duwyne Tollivier (Commandos)
Shielding the prophet's irresistible
Divine intervention to eradicate

Time from repeating its feast
Of this decomposing disease
Feeding off the dreams of others
By revealing its hunger for "White Power"
Southern Traditions:
"White Only"
"Colored Only"
NIGGER LOVER
And some *deem* it only occurred in the South
NOT
South side Milwaukee, Wisconsin

Milwaukee, September 11, 1967 –Having met a shower of bricks and bottles on one of the early marches into the South Side, Father Groppi confers with police and decides to turn back. (Wide World)

Groppi Transferred From St. Veronicas in 1963
He felt it was because he had been to outspoken in denouncing racism and advocating open housing.

Groppi had Mixed Feelings about St. Veronicas at the End
Groppi: "I got along at St. Veronica's all right, but the place was really dead. I'd preach about racial justice, especially in the last year, but there wasn't much going on down there."

Borders

Announcing so every so proudly in front of my seven grade class
Sister Francis Rose stated,
"I was sent to St. Boniface from Appleton because I did
Something wrong"
In my hometown, we had one Negro.
He was our Butler. He was shy and slow, but he was nice colored man."

Now, she taught at a private Catholic school with 60 percent Black
And 40 percent white.

White that were forced to stay
Couldn't afford to move in the suburbs

Cleaning out the debris
The "Ruling Arch" sent the
Their second white best to teach
Anything their conscious could not
Or would not digest

Even Father Groppi was sent from St. Veronica's privilege
White religious community
To an inner city

Half-black Catholic school
Cause he was not "Cool" with racism.

Devoted toward elevating the mind
Heart and spirit of mankind
Father Groppi and the NAACP Youth Council Members
Revoked
The Status Quo
Thus, those punished are *Blind* by their own borders.

Groppi, unlike Most Students at St. Francis, had Great Love for Underprivileged (Summer Camp, ETC)

"A person with tremendous love for the underprivileged. While the rest of the
students were busy during the summer making extra money for the coming year, he
spent his time working with colored children."

Groppi Felt Youth Camp was a Seminal Experience

Groppi:"It was during the last two or three years at Seminary that I began to understand what suffering was. At the day camp, I got to know hundreds of black families and saw firsthand what racism did to people."

Began to eliminate racist stereotypes
Moved by the pain of young black girl being called a nigger
Groppi: "The pain of Jesus Christ as he hung on the cross."

Peggy: "He was moved to civil rights activism by this experience
Attack on blacks was personal to him after this."

"Felt this early contact with blacks was the most important influence affecting his
Civil rights work."

Groppi: "I saw the social suffering and ostracism. I suffered with them and have never stopped suffering

Summer Day camp A Crucial Experience for Groppi
"When we were in Theology, He got involved in with a day camp for Negroes. He spent all his summers working there. He worked with kids all day, the parents all night. For him, it was a day and night camp."

"Almost by accident, Groppi was appointed director..." children ages 3-14 or order
(an "indeterminate number.

Camping Seeds

Who's lacking when summer's fragrance
Radiant's endless sun-ray hours
Challenging young minds
To explore the delightful amusing journey
That
Basketball and baseball
Volleyball and canoeing
Down a river's dumpy path

Camp fire gatherings
Ancient riddles told
Hot dogs toasting
Over cedar coal

Freely embracing
Inexperienced newborn spirits
Broken wings patched with
Homemade band aids.

Parched gardens thirsting to strive
Yet
Rich precious Black soil
Spouting future corn seeds
Black
Yellow
White
Red

Cause someone bothered to feed
Whose womb was lacking
The Sun-rays

Black Web

Blessed be the force that
Penetrates the seed
That webs the Souls
Giving its inner aptitudes that experience
The pain of others

Webbing circles of reflections as it
Mirrors the emptiness of an oak tree
That illuminants the earth as it is forced to swallow
It's true nature to heal and breathe to all that lives

Blessed be the force light that
Penetrates the seed
That webs the Souls
For their journey shall exceed
Feeding
The graves of those that fought
And gave their lives
Be Free.

Groppi Objected to the Minstrel Show at St Francis

Groppi stated, "The central theme of the thing was a caricature of the Negro culture. It portrayed a fat black woman who was supposed to be a harlot. They tried to mimic the black way of speech. It was all a putdown, the worst kind. I almost quit over that. Some of the guys had worked with me in the day camp and had seen the same things I had, and there sat laughing to this caricature of a black woman. It was disgusting. I almost took off my collar."

This & That:
St. Boniface Fall Festival (1960)

Seeing thee so hilarious that you rolled off your chair
As you pointed at two black six years old boys'
Named
This & That's
Black skin ricocheted on a white concrete basement wall
Cause they were so scared.

So scared
This & That's eyeballs popped out of their heads
And floated in midair

So scared
This & That became frozen in space
Like the white ghost
Yet
Screaming
"Runs feets! Runs feets!"

Seeing thee so hilarious that tears rolled down
Your white cheeks forced me to ponder
Why are you adults Christians
Stabbing my little six year old body?

I wanted to *cry*
I wanted to *die*
I wanted to scream
"That's Not Me!"
"We Don't Do That!"
This is *Me* and I am a *human being*!"
Instead
I began *invisible*
As I slowly floated
Way down in a black *bottomless* pit
Hidden in silence
Speechless
Emotionless
Wishing that perhaps the
Thrust in my chest would go away!

Factors Affecting Groppi's Decision to Attend Seminary
1. Read Malcolm Boyd's Are you Running with me Jesus?
2. Saw Gregory Peck in Keys of the Kingdome
3. (while at home in the store during the year after high school)

Groppi:"I was attracted to the priesthood by what I consider the brevity of life, the shortness of it and the desire to make it as meaningful as possible. I had a personal love for Christ, I wanted to follow him, make my life like his."
4. Popularity and joy of youth seemed increasingly meaningful – "There had to be more to life than a basketball, I thought."
5. Realized his dependence on Christ and made a total commitment.
6. His parents did not push him to go.

A Chosen Child

In tune with the silence of the early midnight stars
Quietly, I hummed a song that 'Momma Annie'
Grandmother taught me,
"Amazing Grace"
At 2243 North 13 Street's front porch

Viewing my life in the sky at the age of four
A warm breeze circled around "our" space
The angel sweetly
Song in the mist of blue-black diamond waltzing rays
You my love will ego the *banner* of
Righteousness
Lifting the cloak that blinds the truth
From those whom seek
Equality

Groppi Loved High School
Groppi: "I had a good life while in high school. I played a lot of basketball, and I did some swimming. It was a kind of vacation for four years."

High School: No Vacation

High school wasn't no vacation for me.
Some of the priest and nuns certainly did not
Create a learning environment where little black girls could
Relax
Reflect
And glow with pride.

Perplexed
I asked my Social Studies teacher, Father White
"Where were the Black people?
What did they achieve?
What did they contribute to the United States of America?
AND
Why aren't we mentioned in our textbook(s)?

Shocked and stuttering Father White responded,
Oh, my *"you people"* are the mentioned in the
Social Studies book -
Just look on page 87.

Bewildered
I gradually, yet attentively
Examined the pages prior to arriving
On page 87 -

Refusing to accept the frozen 2 inch picture:
In a 100 acre cotton field

Bent over picking cotton was
A worn out woman dressed in a filthy ragged
Garment
Bare foot
Soil rag tired around her head.

Near her side a half-naked baby sat
Turning dirt for amusement

"This is it! This all there is!"
My young self dared to question.

"Yes, *'your people'* did not do that much"
Proudly, responded the man of Christ, teacher.

Repudiating the latter I crabbed that textbook
Walked to the window
And threw it out!

Crabbing my right ear
Forcefully I was led
To Sister Whitefield's office (principal)
A bottled forced inside bawled,

"Where are my black heroes?
Where are the black teachers?"

DEAF EARS INFECTED WITH DECAY
Blockading
The little black girls' enormous appetite for truth
Forced to witness again
The transparent spirits of so long ago:
Negro
Nigger

So you see high school wasn't, *No* vacation for me

I was too busy knocking down locked doors
And washing disintegrated minds to
Relax
Reflect
And just *tell* the babies the *truth*, so they may *grow* and *flow* with
pride!

Groppi offended by Anti-Italian Prejudice of High School
Groppi:"I remember one day when someone from the Italian
American Civic Association addressed the school. He spoke in very
broken English with a heavy accent. Everyone in the class laughed
but me and another guy. We didn't laugh because that's the way our
parents spoke. My mother didn't even speak English, just Italian.
It hurt."

Groppi Ambivalent About the Link between his Italian-American
Background and his Activism

1). He did see a connection between them.
2) Cautious about comparing the two:

Groppi: "I don't like those kinds of comparisons. Sure we were called
names, but we were still white and that made all the difference."

5 September 1967 (Tuesday) Groppi Led Demonstration to City Hall Prior to Council Endorsement of Mayor's March Ban

Spectators laughed when Dwyer questioned Groppi's Christianity: "Jesus Christ taught us to love our enemies and to do good to those who do harm to us." (said Groppi taught hatred).

1. Mayor Maier did not attend the meeting.

My Muddear Spoke liked an Angel to Me

My Muddear was born and raised *way* back in the woods
On a farm in Pine Bluff, Arkansas
Growing vegetables and raising animals
To put on the table:
Corn
Green snap beans
Carrots
Squash, Collard and Turnip Greens
Chickens
Goats
Cattle
And Pigs

School days were cut short
By third grade
Cause My Muddear was the only child left at home
So My Muddear was forced to help her momma pick cotton, so they could eat.

When
Speaking to my teachers
Or even while grocery shopping out in a crowd
My Muddear's words were musical to my heart

Bringing honey to my soul
Knowing without a doubt that God put that tenderness in her voice:

"*Shelly girl*"
"*Yonder thay go*"
"*Iffen she don't straighten-up real soon y'll*"
Or
"*Commence to hear girl, let me fix tha.*"
"*Ama fixin' that now…*"

So my heart melted and dripped down the sewer
When my teachers laughed behind my Muddear's back
And said she was "ill-bred" because she didn't roll her
R's And T's

Sometimes My Muddear would lower her eyes in shame
Yet I carried her pain and tightly squeezed her hand
And land a big wet kiss on her cheek.
Proudly looking up at her I so sweetly said, as I smiled from ear-to-ear with pride
"This *Here* is My *Muddear*!"

1. Groppi and about 100 marches in the Council Chamber, along with Sidney Finley, NAACP Field Director
2. Groppi threatened violence (at chamber): "The words 'cool it' are no longer part of our vocabulary. We've been using the technique of non-violence. But we're telling them right now we've been most patient. We're getting tired. If necessary, we'll send a thousand people to jail."
3. Groppi vowed to keep marching until open housing is passed."
4. Demonstrators booed Alderman Dwyer when he said, "Surely not a single member of this body is not dedicated to the Christian principle of equality."

(Morning) Groppi Vowed Marchers would Continue: Urged Others to Act
Met with Joseph C. Fagan and others over breakfast
Groppi: "We're going to create pressure. You get that bill in whatever way you want. There'll be no cooling whatever, if we have to send 500 people down...to get arrested."

Milwaukee:
Downtown Jail House Blues

No one bothered to ask me how old are you?
YET
I had just turned 18 years old a week ago on May 4th
HOWEVER
My friends and family said I looked like I was 15 years old.
Now, I tried all the little tricks to make myself look my age:
Thick honey brown liquid make-up
Wide colorful wire loop ear rings -
You know the ones that hand down to your shoulders
And dangled when you walked!
And I refuse to wear a pony tail
Cause that really made me appear even younger
So
I tried all those little tricks
But nothing made me look my age!

After the police grabbed my hand and place it down in a
A small hand pan with black ink
Me and my best friend Mary Childs were sent to the Children's
Detention Center
It was the same place my little sisters' (Glennda, age 12 and Barbara,
14) went when they were arrested.
So Mary and I knew what to expect:
Undress

Shower
The lady guards threw white power on your bodies
Later
Hot Coco & Chocolate Chip cookies
Then we were handed
P'J's that looked like Hospital sleep wear -
Thank God there were no holes.

Bedtime
We were led to separate sound proof cream white color rooms
With army iron twin beds
AND a huge concrete white locked door
With a 2 inch **wired** window
Near the ceiling

Meanwhile
Laying on the army iron twin bed
Mother sleep refused to keep her comforting arms around my tired
teen body
And rock me to sleep
Hours, minutes, seconds passed
Revealing vivid pictures and sounds of my
Family
NAACP Youth Council members
Father Groppi
My Muddear

Ultimately soothing this overwhelmed body
Unlocking Chains
Permitting freedom to buzz forth honey
Sweet melodies
"We Did It!
We Did It!
Me and Mary finally got ARRESTED!
We are Freedom fighting Sisters!"

5: 00 AM
A short stern face white female guard
Rushed through my door
Shouting, "Get Dressed, Let's go!
You have one minute!"

Shocked, in disbelief, I grabbed my jeans, NACCP Youth Council
T-Shirt
Tennis shoes and stepped up behind her.
Escorting me into a small closet
Big enough for a table, two chairs
Sat two white males with suits flipping through a file of papers

As I entered, they ignored my presence.
"Have a sit," directed the female guard.

"What your name? How old are you?
Why didn't you say that you were 18 years old?"
Aloofly inquired the white middle age male police

Bewildered, I replied, "No one ask. My birthday was five days
ago."

Detached as though I wasn't human, the white middle age male
Stacked his paper file, stuffed them in his brown leather suitcase
And indifferently announced,
"Take her downtown to the jail house!"

Oh My GOODNESS!
My heart lost its beat
My confused mind raced:
"If I am taken to the jailhouse downtown,
My Muddear wouldn't know where I am!
How will they know what happen to me?"
How will Father them know where get me out of jail?"

Moments and time spun into speeding blue-pink lights
As the 260 pound white male grabbed my hands and clipped those silver
Handcuffs on my wrist
Water disappeared from my throat.

Step-up, there you go
Downtown to be with the big folks
No freedom songs, not even a note, played its familiar
Melody as the wheels of the "Pappy Wagon"
Bounced rolling freely down the bumpy street
Before the sun to rest on my scared 18 year old cheeks

Again
Left alone in a room with one wooden table
280 pounds white female guards with a long rubber club entered
And stood by the closed door

Looking pass my soul, frankly announced,
"Take off all your clothes
Bend over
Lift up your arms
Lift up your legs
Spread your legs apart
Open your mouth."

Deep down inside my spirit:
Wanted to scream,
My name is Shirley Butler
I am a brave freedom fighter.
INSTEAD

I FOUND MY VOICE
Yet lost my being
i asked, "May, I have a female napkin?"

Laughing with delight, toasting her head to the side and staring
down at Me
The female guard responded,
"This is the jail house, not Walgreens!"

Wet blood siding down my legs with dehumanization
Gradually gathering my soiled jeans and T-Shirt
Down a long dark hall, I was led.

Like on TV, the huge thick silver iron doors slid open
Like a womb to a Coffin
Chills embraced me
Like a raisin burnt by the sun-rays
Dreams deferred
No thick wool gray-black blanket
Lifeless iron army bed could wash away the unfamiliar fear
That laid the parched throat hollow for song.
Yet
The life-blood smothered the nostrils of the mid- damp
Death Cell

LUNCHTIME
I guess noontime
A 280 pound white male opens the door cell and handed me a
Sandwich
Thick rubbery Bologna clogged with white bread
With cold tab water in a medium-size silver can cup.

"Oh hell No You Ain't goin' to eat
That crap!"
My stomach screamed from the bottom of its pit.
Don't you even *dare* mix that stuff with Muddear's
Hot fluffy fried chicken
Double-thick creamy Mac & Cheese
Mouth watery Collard Greens with slow smoked ham hocks
Served-up next to a plate with

A nice-size slice of sweet water homemade cornbread

My empty stomach warned, "If you eat that rubbery Bologna Sandwich, this wills BE YOUR LAST MEAL."

SO
I SAT THERE ON THE IRON BED ALONE
STARING AT THAT *DAMN*
BOLOGNA SANDWICH

The weary lids on my dry eyes closed
As I began to pray,

God, please let My Muddear find me
And come and get me out of the cell hold.
My entire body felt like it as 75 years old.

MINUTES dragged by
Like watching a black army ant carrying a crumb of bread
Across a creek on a slippery stone

Suddenly
Sending thunder bolts to my heart
My entire being sensed a familiar presence
Down the narrow gray-black hall

"Yeah, Yeah, we got it – so she down there?"
Questioned my spiritual brother, Tommy Lee Jr. (Commando)

"After we sign these papers, I must see her," sweetly, yet sternly replied Father Groppi.

Resonating like the thunderous beat of a dejembe drum.
My soul lifted my body with glee.

"*ALLELUIA*" it shouted, "This little child is finally freed!"

Stomp, Stomp, Stomp
The big heavy set feet of the female guard
As she stops at my cell and turned the lock and announced,
"You get your things. It's time for your trial."

**8 Hours and 23 Minutes
Disconnected**

"Be brave, you a freedom fighter"
Don't cry – it's almost over"
Whimpered a little voice deep down inside me

Yet
The Nile River began to over flow
When Tommy Lee Jr. stretched his warm loving black arms
Out and embraced Sojourner Truth's child.

Standing near with the Niger waves waltzing with pride in his eyes
Father Groppi affectively warned,
"Shirley, when we go to trial, *please* don't say anything,
Just say, *YES SIR.*"

Guarding the lamb prior to walking into the slaughter house
The KKK's judge den
Where "Negroes went in and never came out!

Trial
Standing in front of the judge with no limbs
"State your name" the middle age bold headed white judge flatly
stated With *NO*
Eye contact - Busy turning papers
"Where is the policeman that made the arrest of this female
Negro?"

Stepping up front with a wiry smile

"Sir...I mean "you honor" that black girl kicked, pushed me down on the Ground and split in my face" So, I arrested her for disorderly conduct."

Disbelief
My black-brown eyes rolled with disbelief
This policeman was at least 286 pounds and 7 feet tall!
How in the hell could little old me knock him down!
He wasn't even the police that had arrested me.
Clinching my hands together
My eyes read Father Groppi's lips across the court room:
"Shirley, please don't say anything. Just answer any questions if asked with a *YES SIR*"

Amazing Grace
It was amazing grace that reassured
My 18 year old soul
My lips, my tongue froze
An angel in the mist stated,
Sir, she has no prior record, *Not* even a driving ticket
The KKK judge frowned and stated without eye contact.
"Well, this little female Negro is FREE TO GO!"

Released
Shriveling, yet trying to walk out the court room with pride
One tear dropped down my blood stained jeans
Joyful to be able to *walk freely* again

Yet
That night cuddled up in my orange flower blanket
More tears danced down my relieved cheeks
As I hugged my Muddear's sweet laughing voice
Downstairs in the kitchen talking to my father

"Hey, that Shelly girl is just like her momma!"
She ain't afraid of nothing!

That Shelly girl can smell change in the air.
That Shelly girl is the only one out of all my children that were *born free!*"
Smiling, yet safety holding onto my orange flowered blanket
I finally found that lost song in my heart,
"Yeah, I am a *warrior*!
"Yeah, I am a freedom *fighter!*"
"Yeah, I am a *warrior*!"
Yeah, I am a freedom *fighter...Now!*"

Milwaukee NAACP Youth Council Commandos marching on the South Side in Auigust 1967.

From the *Milwaukee Journal*, August 29, 1967; copyright Milwaukee Journal Sentinel, Inc.; reproduced with permission.

Police Hold Back Angry Whites

Police wearing riot helmets and armed with shotguns and tear gas guns held back unruly mobs of whites such as these in the 900 block South Street (upper left), and at South 16th and West Becher Street (upper right).

From the *Milwaukee Journal*, August 30, 1967; copyright Milwaukee Journal Sentinel, Inc.; reproduced with permission.

Friday 8 September 1967: Groppi Spoke to 500 at St. Boniface Rally
Groppi refused to apologize for the rampage at Mayor Meier' office
Wanted mayor to apologize to him
Groppi"The blood of our young men was nearly spilled when we marched to the South side and the mayor never apologized for that," stated Groppi.

Groppi stated that," …Their anger was justifiable."
All marchers told to rest for the big weekend ahead.

Mayor Meier's Office

The major knew the Milwaukee NAACP Youth Council was coming
We had an appointment
But, Lord and Behold
When *We* arrived at his Office
Exhausted and starving for a better life
For black people in Milwaukee
The Mayor slipped out the back door
He didn't even leave us a note.
He was flying so fast out that back
He forgot to close his door.

Baffled
Standing there in the middle of his shinnied orderly office
I thought he was the mayor of Milwaukee
Didn't that include little black me too!
So after a quick minute
We decided to leave him a
A detailed message
One that revealed the urgency to formulate plans to address
The plight too many people were forced to encounter
Just to survive from day to day

So
His papers were hurled around on the floor for display
Like the days of our lives
Trash cans were twirled upside down
Certificates on the wall and pencils were broken
Just like his vow to serve all Milwaukeeans.
Yes
These signs *We* left to say
Us "Colored" folks ain't no joke
Next time 'you is too scared' to meet
Have enough courtesy to leave a decent note!
Thus, it's you who need to make an apology!
"Cause till I is free…you and yours will *NEVER BE!*

Wednesday October 11, 1967 (Day 456) Commandos led Peaceful March
1. Groppi did not march or appear at the pre-march rally
2. About 200 marched to Vel Phillips' home
3. Vel Phillips (clad in yellow Youth Council T Shirt) said: "The whole world is looking at us, and you know we can't fail. And you know, for the first time I feel we are getting close."
    (a) Phillips cautioned against violence: "You've got to keep it cool until then. I don't want to see any more of those knots on your head."

Alderwoman Vel Phillips

Marching in the chilly rain
Lifting our voices to the sky
Singing the tunes from heaven that freedom had bestowed
To every breathing soul

"It May Chill My Body, But Not My Soul"
Old Judge Steffen, Let My People Go!"

Thousands of people let the rain welcomed change
Knocking at their doors
Determined wills to set the crooked pathways
Straight

Lightning rods sparkled as a tiny framed ark
Stood unpaved up against the "Good old white boy's club"
Prevailing and crushing city hall's tradition:
"White Only"- live here
"Black Only" - live there

Standing still

In the eye of the tornado blowing
Ignoring messages sent it in cow manure:
"You are less than my excrement
You *Stop* it nigger wench
Or your neck will hang from a nearby branch"

Refusing to bend to the old wind
Lifting and restoring her wings
Ancestors whispered encouraging words:
"Sock It To Me Black Power!"
Delivering the strength of the ark angels

Guiding the Body
The Soul
And the Mind

We say to you Thank you Alderwoman Vel Phillips
For not compromising our God given
Human rights
Because of you Vel Phillips
Our people may live any place they please:
South side
North side
West side
And
Even the East side, if *We* please!

<u>**Father Groppi and Vel Phillips on Hood of Bus**</u>
Father Groppi, Vel Phillips and Milwaukee NAACP Youth Council/Commandos Members stood on top of a school bus speaking to marchers in 1967.

Photo: Milwaukee Sentinel, Journal Sentinel Inc. reproduced with permission, Wisconsin Historical Society WHi-48419

September 22, 1967 Before Kerner Commission in Washington National Advisory Commission Disorders
Said he could understand the violence of H. Rap Brown and Stokely Carmichael
They had tried nonviolence and had been frustrated by its inefficacy.

H. Rap Brown and Stokley Carmichael

Unbeatable soldiers
Adored by God
Summon up out of the ruins
Bringing spring water, food, and shelter
To those that walked the earth with open abrasions
Arrow spearing coated
Poison tips
Scratching dreams
Congesting the unborn
And controlling

Jurisdiction for
"Yes Sirs"
No Madams"
Is we sick Master?"

No –these ordained Soldiers
Bare arm(s)
Shield the frighten
And fed the empty bellies of babies
The first to say,
How can a child concentrate on an empty stomach?

Embracing the spirits of ancient ancestors
The black warriors organized and stomped

Down selling drugs in the "Hood"

The first to shout,
"Black Power"
Brothers and Sisters we must stand together as a nation for the
people
By any means necessary!
Power to the People
Not to the Government
Not the Republicans
Not the Democrats
But for the people!

These black courageous soldiers stood up like
Black panthers and gave
Hope to those unborn
And even those buried.

Marchers: 13th Walnut

Yes. As a black female
15 at the time
I was out there with my old
Baggie jeans –
Loose just in case *I HAD to RUN!*

Had my favorite holy gray tennis shoes
On my tired feet – ready to
"Kick it" just in case I
HAD to RUN!

Yeah – I had my faded, black NAACP T-shirt
XX Large - just in case
I HAD to RUN
Double-up "drop and roll"

Just in case I HAD to make a quick turn
To avoid your swinging 60 pound black club
Or
Those 30 pound bricks flying at my head
Dying to rob my preteen life

Forbidding me to protect my human rights
Standing to defy rules that
Claim me at only *3/5th* human

Yes. As a black female

66

15 at the time
I was out there with my old
Baggie jeans –
Loose just in case I HAD to RUN!

INSTEAD
I was one of those unarmed women and/or children beaten down
Rolling on our bellies
Under your huge 22 size black shiny army boots

You raked our ribs on the cold dirty concrete ground
 Laughing as though we were
A piece of *Stinky* toilet tissue

Bucking your eyes with a wide queer
Look of bliss
Haunting my mind still vividly recounting your hollow voice,
"Nigger Wrench"
You Say You Want What,
FREEDOM"

What you will *get* and remember is this
Purple blue knot I will brand
On your back

Yes. I was there under your foot
Even today I still say that I will *NEVER* forget
I couldn't RUN
But my soul *soared*
I witnessed my people *rising* up
On the *Mountain Top*!
Destroying your decayed reality!

EVEN knowing that One day, *we* would
Have a *Black President*.

Wednesday August 23, 1967 –Prentice McKinney and Dwight Benning Announced Plans to Picket the South Side
Press Conference at Freedom House
Prentice McKinney said, "We're planning a week-long march on the South Side to see what decent housing looks like. I understand they have green grass down here. We're going to take a look."
He said that marchers would go through September 3rd.
"We want to see if there are places for a black man to live down there."
Groppi might "accompany them."
"Groppi could not be reached for comment."

Southside

Surprised, shocked, flabbergast
Speechless and Confused

Their houses didn't look like nothing that I was told
Nor dreamt
White picketed fences
Hugh mansions on a hill with 100 wide windows
Surround by lawn as green and as smooth as a football field.

Little children dressed in Sunday clothes
With shiny black shoes
Laughing and playing with their bikes
Chasing their spotted black and white dog, *Spot*
Like in my first grade reader:
See Spot Run, Run, Spot, Run
See Sally Run. Run Sally Run.

ALARMED
I saw *DIRTY* windows without curtains
Brown and uncut Grass, if any

No dogs
No children
Paint chipping on old houses
Homes small without porches, no stores, but a bar on every block

Surprised, shocked, flabbergast
Speechless and Confused
What was the Big Secret?
Did They *CHANGE* the Neighborhood?
Cause they knew *WE* were coming.

The South-Siders stood in the streets
Greeting us as we approached,

"Niggers Go Home!"
"Go Back to Africa!"
"Where You Belong!"

I thought in the midst of the shouting:
That's strange – wasn't *their* people who forced us here?"

"White Power Only"
"Dumb Niggers, Go to Hell"

I thought as I walked in shock and fear...isn't this hell?

Oh that's it...they *change* their Southside neighborhood cause they
didn't want Us to *Want* to live there! To see their hidden treasures

Guess what?
It Worked. I didn't *want* to Live There!
So, I asked Father Groppi
Why are *we* marching to live on the *South side*?
I *Don't* Want to *Live There*!

Wisely replying, Father Groppi responded,
"Let's not miss the point –
They said *you can't* and *THEY Ain't God!*

Friday September 22, 19657: Rev Russell Witon Expressed Desire to "Rehabilitate" Groppi

1. Called Groppi's methods: unchristian"
2. "Working for the rehabilitation and conversion of Father Groppi back to his senses."

Unchristian: Father Groppi

Define Christian to me
If you PLEASE:

Affectionate
Charitable
Compassionate
Enduring
And Noble

These were the qualities
That based the heart of Father Groppi

An unconditional soothing light
Glowing through every living creature
Feeding
Clothing
Those poor in spirit
Replacing despair
With *HOPE*

Shouting out for those whom
Voices were chained.

For this Christian
There were no tasks too complex:
Unemployment

Equal pay – bus drivers
Integration - Quality education

Abolishment:
White Only – Eagle's Club
Fair- Housing:
Eradicating – No blacks can live here

So let it be written
Let it be told – Rev. Russell Witon _
Who is the One who needs *REHABILITATION*?
This *Christian's Track record* stands on its own!

Father Groppi during Mass speaks to children at St. Boniface Elementary School in 1968.

From the *Milwaukee Journal*, May, 1968; copyright Milwaukee Journal Sentinel, Inc.; reproduced with permission.

1974: Claimed He Did Not Miss Civil Rights Movement Groppi: It wasn't a lark, Man, it was rough, Nostalgic for jail, being hated?"

Do You Miss the Civil Rights Movement?

That's Right!
It was No lark
It was No Spring vacation
It was No Barbecue cook out!

No, it was like angels coming together
To
Safeguard
Its children from
Flying bricks
Broken glass
Burning tear gas
Even the jaws of wolves
Prowling around in its own vomit
Awaiting to devour its prey:
People of color
Coming together
Demand a better day

That's right – it wasn't No lark
It was No summer vacation
It was more like
PICK-A- NIGGER – TO- COOK ! (PICNIC)

That's Right!
It was no Lark
More like closing your eyes
To drown out the hellish sounds

The smell of blood and scorched human skin

Dreading to take a baby step
Into the bowels of hell
Snakes darting blazing split pooling the corners of
Your flaming eyes
As you attempt to digest the weeping
Sounds of your sisters and brothers
Then and yesterdays

Naked beaten bodies drag
Tar feathered and tagged:
"Nigger, Nigger"
Get Out of Town!
If not your Mama will me the next to feel
The rope around her crown

That's Right
It was No Lark
So I don't miss
My stomach turning upside down
Of forcing myself to hold my pee
Cause if I went to the bathroom on the Southside
While marching
I feared that someone would rape
My soul
Or burn me alive!

That's Right
It was No lark\So I don't miss
Being *TERRIFIED*
MOTIONLESS
Cause my ten year old baby sister's body
Is trembling uncontrollably
Bawling cause her eyes
Are on fire

And her lungs are engulfed with smoke!
Hell No
I don't miss having to encourage my spirit
Everyday
"I would rather be dead then be a slave"
No human being should have to say:
"I will give my life to be FREE
Cause *FREEDOM* is born within *ME*!

Father Groppi arrested while marching for fair housing in 1967.

Photo by Paul Shane

From the *Madison Capital Times*, October 3, 1967; copyright Madison Capital Times; reproduced with permission.

Monday 11 Sept. 1967: Groppi Advised Children to Demonstrate Instead of Going to School
(Speech to Milwaukee Junior Bar Association)

Groppi: He said black and white children got a "third rate" education in Milwaukee - - Whites had no exposure to blacks – Blacks learned nothing of their heritage.

Groppi: "It is important for the black child to learn about himself. By participating in demonstrations the black student can only become a man by learning who he is. He is then ready to go on and study."

Bertha-Mae Whoppi and Me

[*Muddear is an African American name which
means mother dearest]
*(enters with a large white towel tightly wrapped around her head
and speaks with the voice of a four year old.)*
Hi everybody
(Twisting her ear and the corner of her dress)
My name is Mary Ann Lisa.
My Muddear calls me Bertha Mae
(puts her thumb in her mouth and looks down on the floor, sadly)

Me do not like Bertha Mae
So...me calls me Mary Ann Lisa.
(Smiling)
Me is these many years old
(holds up four fingers and rocks from side to side)
Me ain't never see no Bertha Maes on T.V.
If me did
They be all big, dumb and somebody's maid
(Twisting the corner of her dress)

Soooo me changed my name to Mary Ann Lisa
(Smiles and plays with the white towel on her head)
(Looks at the audience with a frown) What you say about my hair?
(Gently stroking the towel) This is my Hair!
(Shaking the towel from side to side) Yes it is!

And when the wind blows
My hair MOVES with it! (Looks at the audience)
Why yall laughs at me?
This is my hair
Yeah it is! And it don't even hurt when my Muddear combs it!
It looks just like the ladies on T.V. too Long and shiny and straight
(Slowly shakes her head up and down)

It bounces too
Just like Mary Ann Lisa
When me uses Prell Shampoo
See
(Walks and shakes her head from side to side)

Even when me bends down to read my favorite book
(Bends down and picks up a book)
My favorite book is Goodie Locks
Oh! (Shocked)
My Muddear brought me a new book
(Sings and shows the book to the audience)
Me got a new book!

This says
(Spelling the letters on the book cover)
Q-U-E-E-N - N-Z-I-N-H-A—Oh looky here
(Points to a picture in the book)
She is helping a bloody, black man take big chains off his feet!
(Sincerely)
WOO-WEE!
That black man looks just like my daddy!

(Spelling)
Q-U-E-E-N - N-Z-I-N-G-H-A

She is sooooo pretty and black and smart
Oh my Goodness looks at her braids
(Puzzled)
I wonder why she isn't on T.V. for little girls like to see.
(Looks at the audience confused)
WOW *(looks at the new book)*

She looks sooooo pretty and she acts like she knows it too!
She looks like just like me
 (Takes the towel off her head and smiles)
My name is Bertha Mae and
I am pretty Too!
(Stands up tall and proud) just like
(Holds up her book)
(Spelling each letter out loud)

Q-U-E-E-N - N-Z-I-N-G-H-A

Heroes Through Whose Eyes?

Once a upon a time in 1964
Back in the 7th grade
At St. Boniface grade school

I was told who my heroes were:
Columbus
De Soto
Ponce De Leon
Cause they explore new lands in the Americas

My heroes, they said:
George Washington

Abe Lincoln
Thomas Jefferson and even
Andrew Jackson

Were my heroes cause, they made America that great country that it
Has become.

But when I eagerly asked, with my hand waving in the midair
Sister, Sister, what did Negro people do?
Sister Francis Rose quickly responded,
Oh, my, let's all turn to page 96.

Hurriedly turning to the back of the history book
I found a tiny photo on the bottom of the page

A Negro woman with a soil, torn scarf on her head
Shabby clothes with a naked "colored" baby
Playing in dirt, near its mother
Picking cotton in a field
Under the photo:
It read: Slave girl, "picking cotton"
Sister Francis Rose's smiled and responded,
"See, there YOU are
You are in the history books too!"

Baffled, I asked,
Are there other achievements that "*Negroes*"
Did in history?
"Oh My child" sister confidently replied,
"They were only slaves, but *they*
We're very HAPPY!"
I felt the blood inside of me
Boil to a peek
So, I grabbed *that* book of lies and tossed it out the
Open early fall window.

Walking in a dazed back to my desk
I swiftly packed my pencil pouch, lunch bag and jacket
And darted out the classroom door – the hall
All the way
6 blocks home!

Heroically singing:
"I am a tree planted by the water, I shall not be moved!"
Star dancing eyes greeted me at the door
My Muddear's proud smiled said,

"Now, Shelly, why did you throw
Your book out the window? -
That book cost $2.00 dollars, you know."

Looking at the mirror
My reflection, I assertively responded,
"Muddear, that book had nothing but white people as my heroes,
With *us* as only slaves
And
You said that we shouldn't lie."

Eye brows rising with dignity
My Muddear said, "Shelley sit and eat your lunch
We are going back with a different book
And *I AM GOIN'* to tell the *REAL STORY!*"

Groppi Was a Prophet in Opinion of Duwayne Tollivier

Tollivier: "I don't believe that the community will ever have a spokesman like that. He woke up the community to the problem that was going on, the racism and the segregation."

Duwayne Tollivier: Commando

Front line
Center stage
Through winter's chills and spring's fresh rain
This commando's wide glee of hope
Made all the rainbows radiant
Unconditional Love
Comforting souls that passed his diamond light

All these ingredients pouring out
From a 6 foot 8 inch 260 pound Man

A commando Giant body frame held
Wings shielding soaring debris
While in harmony his voice
Echoed the strength of ten thousand angel warriors
Resonating:

"Sing a Song, yall
Lift your hand to the sky with pride
Cause I will stomp out the devil with this here
22 size shoe of mine

Front line
Center Stage
As the rainbow waltzed on the guardian of
Truth webbed

The righteous dared to challenge the white "Hoods
That imprisons themselves with
Slithering Tales of the pass:

"I am white; therefore, I have the human right to claim
The life force of all:
The black man
The red man
Even the yellow man

Yet this commando
Took charge
Stood tall like a guarded eagle
Even up against the wall
Tramping down on that spewed lesion:
RAISCISM
Front Line
Center
The Whole Stage
Commando Duwayne Tollivier
You are the one who will *always* be remembered!

**Father Groppi and Milwaukee NAACP Youth Council/
Commandos Members Marching for Open Housing in 1967.**
[*left*, Carmen Carole Butler, author's sister, *center* Duwayne Tollivier,
right, Father Groppi.]

From the *Milwaukee Journal*, May 24, 1965; copyright Milwaukee
Journal Sentinel, Inc.; reproduced with permission.

Groppi's Love for Children Came Through As He Was Driving His Bus in 1983.

He would light-up when children boarded the bus

1979 – Saw Bus as His Church
Groppi: "In a lot of ways, I think of the bus as my church. I miss the opportunities for preaching, teaching, and counseling that I used to have, but this job gives me chances to carry out my ministry in some smaller ways."

Bus Ride: Conversation

Grinning from ear-to-ear
Black stars dancing through thick black trim oval glasses
Thinning, pepper-gray, curly, short hair
Sitting proudly in his dark green county uniform
Controlling the Burleigh Street stirring wheel

Doors swung open
Thick rosy lips parted announcing,
"Shirley, Shirley"
Step right up"

"How are you doing?
"Please come, sit up front, next to me?"

"Where have you been?"
What have you been doing?"
Questions of joy rolling out of his heart

Delighted and surprised
Daughterly responding with deep pride and joy
"Father, I am in my second year in college!"

"I knew it, you better had! You were always so bright!"
Not missing a heart beat
Wise eyes surveyed each street sign
11th, 10th, 9th, 8th, and Holton Street
Frequently stopping to greet a friend:

"Hey there Mr. Brown, You are early today
Did your wife have that baby yet?"

Giving back the warm greeting:
"No, Mr. Bus driver, the doctor say,
She due in two weeks though."

As though Father was speaking to a member of his parish
After Mass, he nodded respectively
"Okay, you take care. I got your family and the new baby
In my prayers

Responding with gratitude, Mr. Brown smiled proudly
As he paid his fair and proceed to look for an empty seat,
"Thanks Mr. Bus driver"

Conducting with grace, style and a fatherly smile
"*Grup*" continued on with his route
Firming griping the turning wheel
With local motor speed
Shoulders set the bus on its pathway
Yet not forgetting the foot prints set a while ago:

"So Shirley, what is your major?
Where are you going to college? "

Familiar with the sprit that planted the seed
Responding was like assuring the spring bud
That it loved bathing in the sunlight

Heart bouncing with bliss
Eager to share the exceptional news

"My major is education
I am going to be a teacher
I am going to UWM"

Radiating at the road ahead
 Like a fulfilled father of his flock
"Shirley, that's wonderful
I am so proud of you
I always knew that you would make an excellent teacher some day!"
I hope that you stay here in Milwaukee
You will make a positive difference."

Inner spirits acknowledged the presence of a Father that changed
The crooked road and made the passageway straight
Vowed to *follow* the trail

Noticing silent wrinkles fading with a smile
I sweetly changed the subject
"So, Father how have you been?"

"Well, I got to go to the doctor and get a check-up
My head has been bothering me a lot
And sometimes it's hard to keep my food down.
The best thing about it is I have lost some weight"

Cleverly changing the subject
Father added,
I see that you have lost your "baby fat"

Aware that Father's loving face had turned pale from apprehension

Comfortably I spoke

"Father, I lost weight cause, I stop eating fried foods
"Father, please don't worry
You will be fine."

Bumpy roads bounced the bus
Yet Father stirred the wheel down the road

Like shaking raindrops off an ancient oak tree
Father affectively replied
"You know Shirley, you and a few others
Still call me Father.

Healing the pain of *"rejection"*
From those that cover with chilly sheets
I immediately stated:

"Father, I know that "they" took away your
Priesthood title
But
You will *always* be my *Father*

Grinning from ear-to-ear
Father firmly held the stirring wheel
As he continued to focus on the cloudy foggy road ahead

In recent years, Father Groppi was a Transit System bus driver and union president.

Photo: John M. Derge

June 1973: Groppi Accused U.S. of Racism in Vietnam
Rocky Mountain
Groppi: "We have slaughtered more Indo-Chinese people than
Hitler killed
Jews. Thirty-six thousand tons of bombs dropped on Cambodia
in April, when
the war was supposed to be over. We have the same attitude
there that we
have here toward non-whites."

War: What's That All About?

Who suffers the most when childless disagreements spur?
Children
Women
And Men

Mostly poor people of color
Families are disconnected
Children are
Lost roaming like scared famished animals
Yellow-grayish rusty open running wounds
Body limbs blowing in the wind
Little bellies oversized
From hunger

Raped tiny wombs
Scared beyond repair
Casted aside like garbage
On an abandon road
Alley
To die
Blind to the prey
Home becomes a vacant cardboard box

Women
Flesh torn open to feed
Those that claim their greed
Land
Title
Filling their loins to satisfy egos' ghostly desires

Men
Eyeballs blown across an unfamiliar dwelling
Pockets stuffed with images of loved ones
Strange beetles nesting inside salty swollen body parts
Fearing Mr. Sleep may rob the will to live
Longing to smell the familiar streets
Home

Upon returning no benefits a greet
Except cold rubber bologna sandwiches
With a band ache and an Anacin to cure
The prerequisite to destroy
Black men
White men
Red men
And Yellow men
SO
Who suffers the most when childless disagreements spur?
Children
Women
And Men

1983-1984: A Top Priority for Groppi was Programs to Increase Bus Safety
      Goal: How to help kids while protecting drivers

Questions: Is That Bus Safe?

Why are children riding school buses without
Safety belts?
Why aren't there No Safety People
On those school buses?
One in Front – to watch little Fred
One in Center – to make sure that LaTonya isn't afraid
One in the Back – to make sure that Jerome doesn't bump his little
head
Do parents have access to the safety school bus rules?
Why are children standing on the bus?
"Pick –up spots before dawn in the morn?

Why are children riding the school bus more than
15 to 20 minutes per day:
To school
From school
Five days a week?
No wonder
Reading, writing, math levels are so damn low
Why can't children just walk across the street
To greet Mr. Knowledge at the front door?
Who benefits from the long?
UNSAFE school bus ride
Oh yeah
THE BUS COMPANIES!

Pre-March Rally of September 11, 1966

1. Groppi cautioned nonviolence: "We don't want anyone running off and doing anything not planned by the Commandos. We want to obtain our end, and that is fair housing."

2. Groppi welcomed whites to "civilized north side": "If the Southside's want to march up here, God bless them. They'll learn that they are coming into a civilized community when they come into the black community."

One Mind: Marching Spirit

Dr. Martin Luther King Jr. was my parent's hero
Malcolm X was mine
At 15, it was very difficult
AGREE:

If someone slapped me
Kicked me
Called me a *NIGGER*
Or even threw a brick at me and mashed
My cute face –
I would just turn my cheek
And *KEEP ON SINGING:*

"I ain't goin' to let Nobody turn me around."

"Oh Hell NO!"
Was my first response at out NAACP Youth Council meeting

Thinking bravely:
If someone even looks at me with the look
Of Satan
I am going to stop

And rock them down to the ground!
Then
From the back of the church basement
Father's familiar voice said,
"Now Shirley, what would you have achieved,
If you stop and rocked them down to the ground?"

"Think about the others marching behind you
Before you
What if they get killed?"
No young lady, you really have to reexamine
WHY you are marching –
To get "Fair Housing"

If you have just a "Temper"
Then you aren't *READY*
For the sacrifice
The dedication
Will-power
It takes to get This *JOB DONE*!"

"Then you should stay home and watch us on T.V."

Embarrassed and confused I asked,
"What if that white power group
Throws glass, rocks at us? What am I to do?"

Lawrence Friend, a wise and devoted commando/president
Stood in the front and replied,
"Let the Commandos watch
For flying glass and rocks,
We *can* block that"

Half satisfied with Lawrence's answer
My fifteen year old mind probed further

"What if that crazy white group of boys
Break into our marching lines and
Start grabbing and dragging
Like they did Mary Ann Childs?"

Supporting Lawrence Friend
Lee McGhee Jr. (vice-president/commando) confidently
Surveyed the brave young freedom warriors
And courageously announced, ""That's why the Commandos are on the
Outside of marchers, to protect you!"
So
You stay with the group marching
Let the Commandos guard your back!"

If you or anybody here has a problem with that
You better not march cause
My life is on the line and
So is everyone else's"

So if you any everyone else wants to practice this
Eye-for-an-Eye sh   t!
You just go on ahead – by yourself
On your one time
Not with the NAACP Youth Council"

"Cause marching with the group is
One Spirit
One Mind
One Goal:
Open Housing"

Immediately – I tied my tennis shoes, lift my head
And marched!

Father Groppi quieted a crowd at an open-housing march just by raising his hand and speaking.

From the *Milwaukee Journal*, August 1967; copyright Milwaukee Journal Sentinel, Inc.; reproduced with permission.

Fall 1967: Groppi Willing to Die for the Cause
Groppi: "I can't think of a more beautiful way to die than by fighting injustice to my black brothers."

Death: Only When

Cometh from my Muddear's loving womb
A breath of life was so adored
Given
To a free beautiful black baby girl

One that claims *no* chains
Only marked with the rays of sunlight
That kisses the ancient wisdom of
The Niger River

Death waits like the ashes of a volcano
To those that temper to chain the
Birth of her footprints

Thursday September 14, 1967: Maier Feared Civil War, defended his Approach, "ordeal that verges on the civil war"
   1. "handful of hate-filled hoodlums responsible"
   2. Asserted that police maintained the peace – "most free city in the world"
   3. Said he would call Guard only as a last resort.
   4. Warned that if "provocateurs, the apostles of violence" persist, it will produce "a violence which will leave death and destruction in its path."

You Is A Hoodlum

According to the Webster's dictionary:
A hoodlum is a "Lawless gang member"
Well, I was out there marching with them too
And I *ain't broken* no laws
Furthermore –
I don't belong to no gang neither –
I don't even have a drivering ticket –

"A *handful* of hate filled hoodlums
WELL
If you call a "Handful"
100,000 determined human beings
Refusing to go One More Endless Day
Without
Food for the baby's bellies
Shelter to shield the chill of the night's hawk
Employment to greet the bill collectors at the door

Dreading -to hear mothers weeping cause her child's
Baby's toe was chewed off by a rat while
She slept in a shoe box
Loathing - Reeking the sight of an erupted sore oozing

Down the side of her 10 year old son's face cause his mother ain't got
no money to take him to the doctor
Can't Bear -To see six school age children share a cold hot dog
For dinner
Hate - To witness hot tears of a grown man cause he
Was told by his employer at A.O. Smith that today
Would be his last day
AND
He has seven children and a wife to feed
Death - Has harbored its presence in the inner city
Too Long
Destruction - Robbing Black people of their dreams:
Equal Education
Descent Housing
Quality employment

HOODLUMS - Mayor Meier is those like "self reflective words"
A lawless gang member
One who stands on the backs of those who
Are the corner stone of the _community_

NO - Mayor – whose image do you see in the mirror?
The hoodlum that devours all and
Distributes to only _what_ reflects it self

"That's the REAL Hoodlum – "a lawless Gang member"

September 22, 1967: Groppi Warned of Violence if Open Housing Marchers Failed (At Rally before Maslowski March)

Groppi: "We have to win here. If we don't, other leaders are coming forth with new strategies that have to be used."

...And We Keep Coming.....

"We have to win here..."
We didn't ask to come ....
You stole and forced us here
Now We Keep Coming....

Benjamin Banneker
George Washington Carver
Harriet Tubman
Sojourner Truth
Mary McLeod Bethume
Charles Drew
Brooker T. Washington

And We Keep Coming...
Mary Church Terrell
Paul Lawrence Dunbar
W.E. B. Bois
Marian Anderson
Zora Neale Hurston

And We Keep Coming...
Marcus Garvey
Dr. Martin Luther King Jr.
Malcolm X
Rosa Parks
Lorraine Hansbury

Ella Fitzgerald
Shirley Chisholm
Bob Marley
Quincy Jones
Shirley Caesar

And We Keep Coming…
Sidney Pointer
Cicely Tyson
Dick Gregory
Octavia Butler
Minnie Butler
Betty Harris-Martin
Lee McGhee Jr.
"Kwame" Loundry Berry Jr.
Sherly Jeter
Ida Royalty
Carole Carmen Butler
Attorney Ron Britton
Vada Harris
Jimmy Harris
Dwyane Tollivier
Tommy Lee Woods
Lawrence Butler
Doreatha Butler
Glennda Butler
Barbara D. Butler
Mary Ann Childs-Arms
Shirley Butler-Degre
Shane Berrywright
LaShon Smith
Linda Smith
Fayemi Jackson
Virginia Stamper
Fred Reed
Oraph Whitney

Jill Scott
And We Keep Coming...

Congressman Gwen Moore
Colin Powell
Ron 'Maulana' Karenga
Brother Booker Ashe
Reuben & Mildred Harpole
Bobby Seals
Huey P. Newton
Angela Davis
Nelson Mandela
Kathleen Cleaver
Barbara Jordan
William Asia Hilliard
Spike Lee
Clayborn Benson
Julie Dash
Bill Crosby
Michael Jackson

And We Keep Coming...
Michelle Obama
President Barack Obama

"We have to win here..."We didn't ask to come....
You stole and forced us here
And *Now* our *aim* is to *WIN*!

Typical Scenes at St. Boniface During Labor Day Weekend 1967

Dick Gregory on St. Boniface steps shouting over Congo drummer who kept time to "swaying, swinging crowds"...shouts of "Sock it to me, Black Power ou, ah, ay."

Gregory said: "Father Groppi has given the Pope respect in our black ghetto for the first time in history."

Mr. Dick Gregory

5 feet and 8 inches crown with woolly
Pepper-gray hair
Stands a mighty *wise* prophet
Who attended more than 10 "Freedom Marches?"

Poised, sharp, and as shrewd as a hawk
This black knight allowed
The winds of the drums to
Carry his huge heart as he stepped into
His words for the people,
"Sock It to Me Black Power - Ou Ha!"

That night *Nothing* was *funny* –
His message penetrated the empty souls
Thirsting for respect
Acknowledgements
That Black people were a force to be *reckoned with*!

No wonder the Pope turned his back to St. Boniface
And closed it down!
Those black folks were *serious* as a *heart attack*!

Father Groppi and Dick Gregory speaking at St. Boniface Church prior to marching in 1968.

From the *Milwaukee Journal*, September 1968; copyright Milwaukee Journal Sentinel, Inc.; reproduced with permission.

Groppi Sat Out 1967 Riots for Pragmatic Reasons

Groppi: "That's all they would have needed is to see me down there: they would have arrested me right away for inciting a riot...we thought we'd just sit this one out."

Protest: Not A Riot

After dropping Mary Ann off at UWM's Johnson Hall
[Upward Bound]
Grup, Lee McGhee Jr., Betty Harris and I
Slowly drove down 3rd street on our way back to
The NAACP Youth Council office

With the van window rolled down
The hot 85 degrees summer breeze
Mushroomed with black- grayish smoke
Engulfed my nose
Forcing my eyes to widen in an unfamiliar fear
And disbelief

Silence ruled as four heads gradually
Arched to witness a nightmare at hand's length:

Fire brazing, glass smashing, wood burning and falling as
Human laughter mixed with screams of terror
While shadow bodies swirled and dashed up and down
Sidewalks

Up in flames:
Chinese food store
George Webb
Red Owl Grocery Store

Radio Shack
Walgreens
Liquor Store
And more…

Questions stampeded my 16 year old mind:
What the hell is going on?
Why are those people running with boxes?

T.V.'s
Radios
Baby strollers
Boxes of toilet paper
Packs of chicken
Bags of fruit

Screaming at the "top of their lungs":
"Black Power"
"Power to the People"

Running with delight tightly holding on for life:
Baby clothes
Baby pampers
Blankets & sheets
Boxes of cigarettes
And loads of bread
Even bags of frozen meat

Yelling and alarming their pass-Byers:

"Girl, go back and get those bicycles for my babies."
"Damn man, they done gone and shot Martin Luther King Jr.!"
"I am tired of this shit:
"Burn it down!"
"Burn it Down!"
"Burn Baby Burn!"

"*I* don't own that store!"
"*You* don't own that store!"
So
"Burn Baby Burn!"
"It's all got to go!"

It's our community
We live here "*they* "don't!"
"Yet, they owe the buildings –
They run the show
Ridiculous *High* prices-
And ain't none of us black folks working here
In our *own* community!
Naw that ain't right!"

"Burn Baby Burn!"
"It's all got to go!"

Satisfied haunting voices whispering its
Purpose for the revolt
Still
Burns the heart of the women
Who witnessed what happens when a blister
Goes unattended:
It boils over!

The Summer of 1967, several days of rioting broke in the black community leaving 3 dead, 100 injured and 1,740 arrested. Then – Mayor Henry Maier declared a state of emergency, issued a 24 hour curfew and got the National Guard to quell the unrest.

1983 – Groppi Feared Gang Warfare
Groppi: "They've got the whole neighborhood terrorized up there, black and white."

Groppi's Response to Tear-Gassing at St. Boniface

Groppi: "I believe ours is the only church in the state that's been tear gassed.
I'm proud of that. When that happened, I knew our church was finally becoming relevant."

Is You Skared Yet?

If you think *we* will *NOT* come to get
You
Cause you are in a church
Think Again –
We did it before:
4 black baby girls' body parts went
Soaring to the ceiling with the debris
Now do you remember me?
Is you skared Yet?

While you are in that church: St. Boniface
Meeting to pray
To strategize for the next day
I'll be outside lurking in the brushes
Scoping my prey
Is you skared yet?

I'll send my smoke-bombs
Swirling like a boa
Slithering and claiming every crack and corner
Aiming to burn the black off your skin

Blistering your souls' desire to think
You human, thus you be free
Is you skared Yet?

I'll trail you like a wolf, waiting for the moment
To devour your dreams
Everywhere you go, I'll be there:
Flashing pictures of you:
Your momma
Your sisters
Your daddy
Your brothers
Even your dog!
Is you skared yet?

I'll drive my car up on the sidewalk
Ignoring any grass or stop signs
Grab your arm and push you into my car
I'll flash pictures of those hoodlums
You meet with
And tell you that you better tell me their names
If you don't I am going to take you to jail
Or
I'll bomb your whole house
While you and your family is a sleep
Is you skared yet?

If you missed the bullets dashing through
Your house
And you catch a glimpse of me
Driving away from the scene
Like a manic
You better NOT call the cops
Cause I will come back
And take out your entire freedom loving family
Is you skared NOW?

Without Proof, Opponents of Groppi Alleged Sexual Misconduct

"The sexual prowess so often attributed to the black man was transferred to the personally austere priest."
Cab driver: "That guy spends all day screwing those nigger boards.
That's why he's always marchin'

Sexual Prowess:
Reverse

Some minds are as tiny as the hole in a needle
Inherited from miniature empty souls
Barren as an icy pine tree
With no purpose
Other than to poke
Their rusty needles at my rose brushes

Nicknames for Groppi – Fall 1967

"Ajax the White Knight" (Some blacks called him this)
"Grup" (used by close friends)

'Grup'

Father James E. Groppi was "cool" like that
Down with
Devotion
Dedication
Love and Respect

Grup's heart was big like that
Sharing everything he had:
A cigarette
A slice of bread
His glasses if he thought you couldn't see

Grup was that <u>father</u> to all the children who sought
Love,
Understanding
And Patience

Grup was the <u>teacher</u> to all who seek
Knowledge
Wisdom
And Purpose

Clapping "off-beat" to Aretha Franklin's
R-E-S-P-E-C-T
We would be clapping and singing to the *right*
Grup be clapping and singing to the *left* – with a wide grin
Trying with all his might to find the middle tune

Yeah – *Grup* was "cool" like that
Boiling up a huge silver pot of
Italian sausages in the rectory's kitchen
From his parents' grocery store
Grup would raise, his voice and shout
"Eat-up yall– don't be shy"
It's enough for everyone!"
And no one was allowed to lay down a dollar
Yeah, *Grup* for "cool" like that

Driving up in the heart of the "Ghetto" in his
Beige-Brown Station Wagon
Bring needed families carts of
Food to nourish the soul, the body, and the mind
Clothing to shield the chill from Mr. Jack Frost
While:
In *Grup's* presence even a child's opinion
Was sacred
Grup enjoyed planting:
Seeds and watching them grow
Yeah – *Grup* was "cool" like that!

Groppi's Conception of the Radical Christ Paralleled the Depiction of Christ at Immaculate Conception Church in Bay View

Groppi: "…a suffering Christ, a grimaced Christ with aquiline features and a crown of thorns, a crucified Christ."

That's Not My Jesus!

Having a difficult time looking up and praying to a
Blond
Blue-eyed
Jesus
He don't even look like me

This strange-man nailed on a cross
He looks like he is in pain with a
Thorn for a crown
How will he hear?
See
Me
Feel my pain
Know my dreams
He way up there in
HEAVEN
Above the clouds
Too high up for little black me

How is he going to recognize my plea?
When the ones down here on earth
That looks like thee
Hate
Despise Black people like Me

Hummm…
Still having a difficult time looking way up there
Praying to a
Blond
Blue-eyed
JESUS!
Who seriously doesn't look nothing like me!

1967 – Groppi Wanted an Institutional Church Building

"Although Father Groppi was in a situation where he could operate with relative freedom he still yearned for a parish of his own that he could operate independently. In late 1967, he said he wanted a church that could function as more than just a place of worship, a church that would have kitchen facilities where the poor could get meals, and a place that could serve as a haven for people with no other place to stay. "If I needed the room, he said, "I could take out the pews in the church and put up some beds."

Aukofer, Frank (1968).

Freedom House:
15th Vliet Street

Lee McGhee Jr., Betty Harris, Mary Childs and I
Enthusiastically rolled up our NAACP T-shirts
And blue jeans
With a huge silver pail of Tide Washing Power
Pine-Sol
Torn rags – bending on our knees
Feverously scrubbing the entire
Freedom House:

Windows
Floors
Walls
Kitchen cupboards
Bathroom
While a million fat roaches angrily
Packed their suitcases and scurried across the street
To find somewhere else to sleep

There were so many of those little brown creatures
We made sure that we covered our heads
Just in case they jumped in to make a bed

Even the rats whose swollen bellies from last night's treat
Held a conference and agreed
It was time to relocate
Out the back porch – down the alley they fled
Leaving a three leg dark-brown sofa
Supported by an orange crate
Four fold-up garden chairs
And one donated red and white cooler
To chill water and baloney
Was the only furniture we had

A rusty silver-gray pot was heated
On the stove for coffee and for an occasional bath
When the gas was on
During group meetings in the late fall or winter months
Everyone kept their coats on just to keep warm

It was so cold those massagers
Circled
And floated in midair
Warming an occasional snack:
Buttered bread
Strawberry/blueberry jam
This was shared after
The gathering of friends strategizing for a better day

Beginning and closing with spirited voices
Lifting and filling the small crowded living room with:

"You May Chill My Body, but Not My Soul…"
Thus, without a doubt
This Freedom House was a haven for so many

That lacked:
Jobs
Shelter
Food
And Hope

Waltzing its purple rays over those whose journey needed a
Place of warmth
Laughter
Tears
And a haven to hold onto to dreams

A Policeman armed with a riot gun stood guard while firemen fought the fire in the flaming Freedom House, 1316 North 15th Street.

From the *Milwaukee Journal*, August 30, 1967; copyright Milwaukee Journal Sentinel, Inc.; reproduced with permission. - Journal Photo -

May 26, 1968: Groppi Felt Blacks Had Right to Lead Their Own Revolution
Groppi: "Black people have the right to lead their own revolution… this is essential."

Rise-Up Black Leaders

I need a black, nappy- headed, wide nose, thick lip hero
Someone who looks like me
Someone who wears the same black skin as I
Today
Tomorrow
And all my yesterday years

Someone who has lived with the same preordained
Mental, Physical, Emotional, and Psychological scars
Of slavery

Forced to walk the earth judged by the color of their
Skin
Not by one's character
I need a black, nappy- headed, wide nose, thick lip hero
Someone who looks like me

Someone *Bold* enough to scream, yell
Let's change this *shit*!
Let's organize and tear-down this
"This White Power Only Mentality"

Someone who refuses to lower his head to the ground
With shame

Someone who refuses to be comfortable with:
"I got mine, you get yours!"

I need a black, nappy- headed, wide nose, thick lip hero
Someone who looks like me

Someone who would stump-down on
RASICISM
And force change by any means necessary:
Picketing
Marching
Sit-ins
And Striking....
To secure the rights for all living things
Now and for the babies of tomorrow
So
Our children will be able to shout
From Mount Everest in Asia to
Mount Yasus in Ethiopia

Bequeathing their echoing voices even
In the low streams of the muddy Mississippi river
Witnessing the written words that:
Black people were not just:
Fried chicken
Watermelon eating people
Running around too scared to speak up
Stand-up against the injustices forced upon them

I need a black, nappy- headed, wide nose, thick lip hero
Someone who looks like me

August 1968: Groppi lauded Viet Cong at Milwaukee Hiroshima
Day Rally for Peace

"Father Groppi Lauds Cong."

1. The Viet Cong Struggle courageous
   Groppi: "Whether we like it or not, their struggle is much
   more courageous than our own struggle when we were
   trying to get England off our back"

2. "Nothing short of heroic"
   Struggle to get "Foreign persons off their land."
   Similarities between black and Viet Cong struggles (White
   police, like American troops in Vietnam (completely
   "infiltrate" the community.)
3. Denounced the Viet Nam war
   Groppi: "Black people killing yellow people for white
   people who stole land from the Red people

Struggle: Viet Cong

Let's bow our heads
And give praise to the women and men
Who gave their precious gift
life
In the Viet Cong war
That pinned Black men to kill
Yellow men
For the *White* men
Who stole the land from the *Red* men

Oh, please excuse me
"I meant for a 'fair trade'
Land for exchanged for a few

SHINY things

Let's bow our heads
And give praise to the women and men
Who gave their body parts
A leg
An eye
An arm
Or a knee
In the Viet Cong war
That pinned *Black* men to kill
Yellow men
For the *White* men
Who stole the land from the *Red* men

Upon returning home
They encountered
"Negroes aren't 'really free'
You can't live here,
My *god* what will my neighbors think?"

Let's bow our heads
And give praise to the women and men
Who gave their precious gift of *life*
In the Viet Cong war
That pinned *Black* men to kill
Yellow men
For the *White* men
Who stole the land from the *Red* men?

July 13, 1970: Groppi Frightened by Death Threat Groppi to Cullen
Groppi: "The police were here this afternoon. They said that they had reliable information that someone from the Minneapolis St. Paul area was going to kill me. They were just coming to warn me. I've had that before, but this one was a little chilling."

Knock Knock: Mr. Death
(Philadelphia NAACP Conference – 1968)

At the gathering of great minds
Mr. Death announced his need to make an appearance
As a Chicago Black Nationalist male

A Black pistol pointed at my temple
"Say it ain't so sister"
"Say it ain't so –"
You refuse to follow a white man – a white priest
Or I will blow your brains out!"

Locked in a hotel room with eight black brothers
And three other *captured* Milwaukee NAACP Youth Council Members

Outraged they were with those *"Uncle Toms"* from Milwaukee
Hiding behind the tail of a white man –
A white leader

"Sister, I said, say it *"Say it ain't so sister*
Say it ain't so –"
You ain't going to follow that white man
No more or I goin' to shoot
You dead!"

"*Brother*, I said, to you I am *already* dead if you want
To kill, your *sister* -
This sister is fighting by any means necessary to free
Our people from oppression!"

Knock, Knock
Mr. Death recognized the spirit of truth:
"Okay – Okay sister I see your point!"
And lowered his pistol
But
You and your homeys better get-up out of here
Before I *forget* what this *struggle* is all about
You and *Me* being *FREE*!"

January 30, 1969: Groppi Admitted That He Was "No Longer Needed"
Due to Maturation of the Black Movement in Milwaukee

Groppi: "They are now organized into a power group and so, it's been a process of self-elimination. They no longer need me."

Saw his role as one of "developing indigenous black leadership."

Asante Sana ('Thank You') Father Groppi

Thank you Father Groppi for giving birth to my black beauty:

Black face
Nappy hair
Dark Brown eyes
And thick brown lips
Cause before you came
I knew of only shame

Thank you Father Groppi for giving birth to my being:

Cause it was you who told me that I ascend from
A Great Nation of people:
Queen Sheba
Queen Nzingha
King Solomon
Crispus Attucks
Benjamin Banneker
Harriet Tubman
Sojourner Truth
And Frederick Douglas

Thank you Father Groppi for allowing me to express myself

Cause before I met you I was told that I was a NIGGER
And that my thoughts didn't matter:
You took the lid off the box
When you said:
"You have the right to say that you want descent housing
You have the right as a human being to go to any school
You choose, where there are "quality teachers and
Current textbooks and the latest equipment"

Thank you Father Groppi for telling me that Black history

Should be included in my textbooks
And I have the right as a human being to demand that
The true history of America should be told
Cause if you excluded the Black men
Then history is a LIE
It becomes HIS-Story
Not the REAL Story.

Thank you Father Groppi for loving little Black me

When I fought with all my heart – for a week
To refuse your love
Cause of your white skin
However:
With your unconditional love
Patience
Understanding
Your persistence, shaped and mold me into
A humble, loving, wise, strong, determined
Human being

Asante Sana, 'Thank You' Father Groppi…..
Asante Sana, Thank you Father Groppi…..
Asante Sana….

Father Groppi wearing sunglasses with members of the Milwaukee NAACP Youth Council singing freedom songs on the steps of St. Boniface church outside in 1968. (*Center* female in the back, Shirley Butler-Derge, author, *right front*, Velma L. Coggs, and *right* male, Kenneth McGhee). *Courtesy of Wisconsin Historical Society Museum ID#5295 1968.*

Thursday January 16, 1969: Groppi Spoke at Wittenburg University, Springfield, Ohio (one minute speech)

"Groppi Defends Violence, Power."
Groppi explained the reason for the one minute speech at the University of Dayton on Friday 17, January 1969

An Unnecessary Black University Experience (1970)

First
I called, and left written messages in my advisor's mailbox
Requesting a meeting to discuss the next courses I should take to
Complete my certification requirements –
She agreed

Second
Upon my arrival to my advisor's office
The door was *closed* and *locked* with a written message
On the door knob,
"Sorry"

Third
After at least six arranged/canceled *"Sorry (s)"*
Her door was partly open for a one minute meeting:
With her finger pointing signaling for my entrance

"I'm on the phone, let's make it quick!
What can I do for you?" she crossly asked

Determined to seek her assistance, I replied,
"Well, since you were *assigned* to be my advisor
I am here for some advice –
What classes should I take next semester?"

Holding the phone in her hand
Gnashing her teeth, she stated,

"Well there Missy, IF YOU Make it to next semester
Just choose your courses from the brochure"

Refusing to accept a low image of myself
I quickly said
"With my 3.8 GPA
I definitely plan to *stay*"

Frowning as if irritated, she quickly responded
"Well, like I said before,
I'm on the *damn* phone – leave and *closed* the door!"

Fourth
Our next meetings continued just as previously
It was time for me to student teach
My advisor made arrangements to come and observe me
While I taught a group of 40 all white students –
NEVER
Looking up from her pen
Noticing digest on her pale face – she abruptly gathered-up
Her purse
Notepad and stormed out the classroom door

Leaving behind a wrinkled note on my desk:

Appearance – A   Lessons Plans - B

Informative – C

Direct Teaching – B-

Preparation – B-

Overall Grade C-   *P.S. You only had one piece of chalk on the blackboard ledge.*
Last
I called another arranged meeting with my advisor and the
Grievous Committee to demand an explanation and removable
Of the C- Grade
During the meeting, her boy friend, the chairperson on the
committee asked:
"Will this C lower your GPA? –
Because *we* are aware that you are on a fellowship
Which you have to maintain a 3.5 to *keep*"

Confident, I answered
"No, I have all A's in my other four classes"
"Then, it will remain a C." flared the chairperson

Outraged, confused and crushed
My body carried my soul through the Student Union
Doors and I sat on the cold concrete steps
Until the Burleigh bus came to take me home

Two weeks later I received a letter from my advisor
That stated,
"Don't you *ever* return to UWM *again*! Especially in the
Exceptional Education Department – thus you are *No
Longer* registered"

I took a short needed break with much relief
Return within a year and got my Masters in that *same* department!
She remained on paper –
But I got my advice from God
One year, seven months later my advisor had a stroke and died.

September 4, 1967: St. Boniface Like Brown's AME Church in Selma (Labor Day Weekend)
1. "refuge, rally hall, medical station, housing and transportation bureau, and cafeteria
2. Open 24 hours per day
3. Physicians and nurses on duty to treat foot blisters, cuts, bruises, muscle strains
4. Many donations of food and money
5. Extra phone numbers installed
6. Groppi saw the parallels to Selma
    (a) Nightly marches
    (b) Many outsiders, especially clergy
    (c) Sleeping on the church floor, etc.

7. **A refuge for activities (Barjene)**
"It stood for civil rights. All the activities from all over the country knew there was a refuge here."

St. Boniface: Selma

Now at the age of 50
Flashing photos of St. Boniface during the 60's
Have pasted
My eyes' visions of vivid pictures:
My body still carries fragrances:

My mind still recalls:
Peanut butter sandwiches
Thin Baloney and cheese sandwiches
On White Wonder Bread
Washed down with cold white milk
After every march
In the basement cafeteria

My eyes still see vivid pictures:
My body still carries fragrances:
My mind still recalls

Refuge – homeless
Young black males' sleeping on the cold concrete floors
Wrapped-up with a donated grey-wool blanket
Comforted from the 10 below bitter winter frost
Or the windy raining chill that bounced against the
Window panes
Or
Sitting on the white sparkled titled meeting floor
Sharing stories:
Laughing and bragging about what they did
And how they did it
While marching – way until the next morn

Only on weekends – cause Muddear said-
Shelly, Cal, Bobbie and Glenda must leave by 10:00PM
In-order to get up for school the next day

My eyes still see vivid pictures:
My body still carries fragrances:
My mind still recalls

Rally Hall
Commandos and Grup often extending the strategy plan meetings
Way pass two- three hours
In the church basement
While the NAACP Youth Council members
(Me, Betty, Pam) spoke and/or song
Words of encouragement to visitors
And/or waiting 1000's of marching
Men
Women
And little children

All dressed in gear
Umbrella – if it rained
Walking shoes – for long distances
Carrying
Posters/signs made from the previous night:

Equality for All
Stop Busing
Integration not Segregation
Stop Job Discrimination

My eyes still see vivid pictures:
My body still carries fragrances:
My mind still recalls

Resonating songs of hope
Moved the stomp of feet
Hands clapping the circle of expectation of
Change:
"I Shall Not, I Shall Not Be Moved
I Shall Not, I Shall Not Be Moved
Just Like A Tree Planted By the Water…
I Shall Not Be Moved."

In agreement with the song leaders
The frequent respond from the audience:
"Amen – You Go Girl!
That's Right!"

My eyes still see vivid pictures:
My body still carries fragrances:
My mind still recalls:

Medical Station
Even nails stuck in ones holy shoes
Were attended by a red head doctor after marching

In the medical station in the church basement

Transportation
And in the mist of the closing of the day one
Would hear,
"Let's go!" Let's Go!"
Disappointed teens would regrettably say *"Oh NO!*
To Sylvester Williams' (Commando) familiar alto stern voice

So clearly the teens knew:
No stopping at McDonalds
For a late juicy cheese burger with popping hot French fries
Oh *No, Not* with Sylvester
It was always -
Straight to our parents' front door
Cause Sylvester never broke a rule

St. Boniface
Yes – it had it all:

Love
Friendship
Shelter
Comfort
Food
Laughter
Despair
Security
And Dreams

Weber: "He was considered very devout by most of the parishioners who knew him. Later when he started leading the marches a lot of them felt, 'something must have happened to him. Something got hold of him and turned him bad."

Not Bad: But Mad

Some People Say:
I changed for the better:
A brand new car with
Air conditioner
CD player
4 doors with baby-blue leather interior
Nothing else didn't matter no more….

Some People Say:
I changed for the better
A two story mansion way up on a hill
With a black French iron fence
Surround by a garden full of purple and white flowers
Nothing else didn't matter no more…

Some People Say:
I changed for the better
Candle-light dinning in the fancy restaurants
Thick juicy T-Bone Steaks
Large lobster-tails dipped in hot butter
Washed down by white chilled wine
Nothing else didn't matter no more…

HOWEVER:

Special People Say:
Sharing a piece of bread
With a hungry child
Did Matter

Special People Say:
Giving a worried mother money for her rent
To keep a roof over her family's head
Did Matter

Special People Say:
Providing a warm, and safe place for those who
Slept in a rat infested damp alley
Not fit for an animal
Did Matter

Special People Say:
Telling a nappy head
Black five year-old child
That she has beautiful skin
And that she is lovable
And made in the image of God
Did Matter

Special People Say:
Teaching Black youths that they must
Stand, shout and wisely
Advocate for their human rights
Did Matter

Naw – I ain't gone BAD –
I'm just MAD as hell!

Example of Dick Gregory's Humor Fall 1967
Gregory: "Just when I was getting ready to dislike all white folks, along came Father Groppi and I had to postpone it another month."

Postpone: Surprise

Here on this here earth
There will be many battles over:
Food
Water
Shelter
Education
Employment
Religion
Land
And Identity

So when these struggles present themselves:
The *race* that *bleeds*
Must *lead*!

From this strategy *spawns*
Contagious leaders
Then the war is truly won!

Groppi: "I reacted violently on some occasions. I did. I almost killed two policemen in Milwaukee one night because they were following me. They followed me for three months – everywhere I went- to my mother's, to the restaurant, in and out of church. I'd take the kids home in the parish and when I'd drop ['em off, the damn cops would come up and take down their addresses]. Fifteen and 16 year old girls. They followed me one night and I blew up. I threw the car into what I thought was reverse and stepped on the gas and smashed into the road. I missed."

Peggy: (He hit "park" by mistake)

November 5, 1985: Ald. Richard Spaulding on Groppi's Continuing Unpopularity
"I believe he had just as many enemies as he had friends. People out there hate him as much as love him."

Police Please!

So – tell me something-
Who *is* you pretending to be protecting
With your 6.8 foot tall
290 pound white male self?

Prowling around
My 16 year old daughter
Day and night
Who you trying to fright?

Following her everywhere she goes:
Church
Library
School
Freedom marches

Even to the candy store

Got my baby girl so upset
She sat me down the other day
And told me so

So – tell me something-
Who *is* you pretending to be protecting
With your 6.8 foot tall
290 pound white male self?

My daughter don't even have a traffic ticket
Too young to drive
So I telling you something
This *here mess* just not *jive*!

Police Please!

Enemies

My Muddear use to say -

Jesus had a whole bunch of Enemies
Look what they did to him –
If they did that to Jesus
What makes you think *you*
them same Enemies ain't after you?
Why should you be *spared*?

Groppi: The Northern "Macho Image" Made Violence More Likely in North

Groppi: "You have a macho image to deal with in the North that you did not have in the South. A lot of the guys I was organizing had been fighting in the streets, since they were born."

Macho Man Walking

Strolling down 3rd Center Street with my wide brim
Black hat
Tilted to the side
Just enough to cover my left eye
Covered with my black square sunglasses
Even if it's cloudy outside:

Strolling down 3rd Center Street with my wide brim
Black hat
I still got my wide smile
With my dance toes
Rocking and swaying
Like I got a million dollars in
Empty pockets
And I be a walkin' like I *gots* important places to go

Strolling down 3rd Center Street with my wide brim
Black hat –
Jumping real quick with my homeys
Whistling tenor tunes along with my brothers'
Favorite freedom shout outs:

"Hell No…We Won't Go"!
Hell No….We Won't Go!
Down with old Jim Crow!"

Strolling down 3rd Center Street with my wide brim
Black hat –
Ignoring the whimpering sounds that hunger made
Because my belly hadn't eaten since two nights back
When I stood in line for 8 hours hoping that I would get
A chance to work today
Only to find that food stamps was what they gave us instead of
pay

Still – I rise each and everyday
Even if it means just to Stroll
With stuffed cardboard underneath by feet
Down 3rd Center Street with my wide brim
Black hat –
In my worn-out dusty shoes
To cover the beaten soul from the hailing rain

You See -
Strolling down 3rd Center Street with my wide brim
Black hat –
With a dance step
A tune in my heart
A smile on my face
Lets me know
I am somebody
Yeah I am a man
Not a Macho man
But A real man

Peale Opposed Groppi, September 15, 1967
"I recognize his right to do that, but it grates on me to see clergyman conducting themselves in anger."

Poor: Washington D.C.

Frozen in space my heart lost its beat(s)
Upon my first view of Washington D.C.:

Manicure green carpet grass
Lily of the field
Ruby roses
Artfully displayed among 20 or more cherry blossom trees
Welcoming you to an enormous
White mansion protected by a grand iron
Black fence with arrows on the top

Yet in a 4 block radius
Black and brown queens claimed the
Moon-Night and the crack dawn
Fully clad in scarlet translucent clothes
Thick pancake make-up
With mustache needles poking out through *tried* skin
Lined with ruby-red lipstick

Parading up and down Y and U streets
Coco square silk stocking hailing their prey for exchange:

Quick love for food
Quick love for shelter
Quick love for medicine
Quick love for clothing

Frozen in space my heart lost its beat(s)
Upon my first view of Washington D.C.:

Just around the corner
Bare waist 3- 4 year old babies
Drown with stink from last night's
Body waist
Nose dripping and swallowing pea green cold
Wailing hands extended
In midair soliciting:
"Lady, can I have a penny?"

Frozen in space my heart lost its beat(s)
Upon my first view of Washington D.C.:

Those hollow ancient little eyes begging for a chance
To-Live- to Be
Still are frozen in my heart
My spirit
My mind
Questioned:
"How can this be?"
Had "they" forgotten about *those* people
JUST
Around the corner?"

Frozen in space my heart lost its beat(s)
Upon my first view of Washington D.C.:

Oh how my soul shrieked at those who lived in the "people's"
White House:

Stomachs bursting from yesterdays:
Easter's feast
Baked honey ham and colorfully egg hunts
While
Prostitutes, Queens and *Starving Babies* dare dream
Only a few blocks away
1967: Father Groppi Eldred Lesniewski Afraid to Join Groppi on March (Groppi, trembling, had stepped out of the crowd and asked Lesniewski to join the march)

"I said, 'No' I'll remember that. I think he realized he needed his brother priests with him. But he was in a situation where I thought it would be very dangerous for me to accompany him."

"I wish that we could have been friends. He was one person I tried to work with, and I couldn't."

Yes! I Did!!!

Few people, not all
But some people yearn to have the opportunity
To walk with *Jesus*
To help carry the load -
I Did!

When He asked me to give:

Strength
Unconditional Love
Comfort
Guidance
Hope
Encouragement
To others
I Did!

When He asked me to undo the veil
That shield my eyes from the truth
I Did!

So when my curtains close
And I am back at home
I will be able to proudly shout!
I Did!
"*Yes*, I did Father!"
"*Yes*, I did Father!"

Father Groppi (left) marching and singing freedon songs with children from St. Boniface Elementary School in 1966.

From the *Milwaukee Journal*, October 1966; copyright Milwaukee Journal Sentinel, Inc.; reproduced with permission.

1967: Groppi Claimed Milwaukee Race Situation as bad as the South's
Groppi: "Milwaukee has always been just as bad as anything in the South.
As far as race relations are concerned, I think Milwaukee is about as bad as any city
you'll find anywhere, including Jackson, Mississippi."

Racism: Catholic High School

"Nigger you should be mighty grateful that *my* parish
Generously gave *you* a four year scholarship
To attend our catholic high school"
So
"You better *Stand*, raise your *Hand*, and *Salute* to the
'Pledge Alliance' to the American flag!"
Father Matthews shouted with an infuriated voice
From the front of the classroom
During catechism class!"

Slowly shaking my head with disbelief from side-to-side
 Dismay, I forced myself to shout
"No"
To a *holy man*
Now I thought
I was sure stuff going to
HELL

Even through streaming hot tears
I heard my confused mind
Say:
I can't *believe* this is a
Priest –
A man of God called me a *"nigger"*

As I collected my books and swiftly walked out of the classroom
Tears blind my path
Yet
Slowly I led one foot in front of the other to
The 76th street bus stop:
There I sat alone on the moist green bench
The only sound I became aware of was the
Black birds chirping in the yellow-red trees just
Above my head:

Their voices seem to say:
Remember what Muddear told you the other day
About in Pine Bluff, Arkansas
When she was growing-up, there were signs everywhere
That read
"Coloreds Only"
And
"White Only"

But, still choking through tears of shame
And shock –
I silently pondered:
If they didn't what me here at their lily white
Catholic high school –
Why didn't they just hang-up signs saying
"NO Niggers Allowed"

Suddenly a rain drop fell on my face –
I thought – wait a minute
I didn't see No signs that read,
No Shirley's Allowed
Only Niggers -
So
I gathered up my books
And marched back to

That lily white catholic high school!
I Waltzed back up to Father Matthews and confidently shouted,
With all the strength within me:

"My name is Shirley
I am not a NIGGER
You are the NIGGER
For calling a child a dirty name!"

January 6, 1974" Groppi Calmer and More Reflective
Groppi: "You can't champion every cause…if you shout all the
time, people don't here you anymore."

Journey: Earth Zone

On this here planet Earth
Nothing is perfect – except death
Until that end moment –
I will absorb and devour
The mind's images and fragrances of the universe:

Images – fragrances:
The breeze of a weeping willow tree
The rhymes of the water waves
The multiple sparkles of the rainbow's bubble
The smooth fur of a kitten
A wet kiss from a lover
The birth of one's first child

The fresh oatmeal smell of a newborn's breathe
The humming of a mocking bird
The giggles of a child
The tears of joy from a new grandparent
The sight of your child (*son*) hitting his first home-run
And running to the third base first-
The summer's heat on your back at the fishing banks
And your bobber bounces up-and-down.

Images - Fragrances:
The mouth watering taste of fresh hot fried crunchy catfish
Thick creamy Mac & Cheese
The savor of tulip and mustard greens with onions/ham hocks

And homemade Icebox Lemon Meringue pie

Sizzling hot fried chicken with Louisiana hot sauce
Colby cheese and wheat crackers`
Washed down with
An icy cold glass of Red Cherry soda
Then
Sit back, pull up my sleeves and strike –out the next struggle(s) that
life brings.

Before Marches, Groppi Exhorted His Marchers to have Courage/to be Willing to Die if Needed Be

Groppi: "If you're afraid to go to jail or afraid of tear gas or afraid of dying, you shouldn't have come here tonight. Some things are more important than life. We are not afraid of dying if that's what it takes to guarantee that the black man's rights will be respected in Milwaukee."

No Turning Back

Mr. James Brown proudly shouted
"Say It Loud, I am Black and Proud
So – open up the door
I will get it myself!"

Those courageous words encouraged
And motivated
Thousands of Milwaukeeans to march -
To walk in the streets
Day or night
Rain or shine
Even through the beasty winter snow
Knowing that it might just be the last time going –
Last time to breathe
Or bathe under the sunrays
Swallow your last meal
Walking with your life-long friends
Feeling the warmth of their hand as you march
Though the devil's diner on the Southside
Of Milwaukee, Wisconsin

Naw, there ain't No turning back to:
"Nigger go back to Africa

"A Good Nigger is a dead Nigger!"
Back to:
A endless toothache cause you have
No dental insurance
Back to:
Torn and/or outdated textbooks
Or teachers calling you black coons
Back to:
Sleeping in alleys and/or park benches
Back to:
Riding unsupervised school buses 4 hours a day –
When there is a school across the street in your own neighborhood
Naw I ain't afraid of no tear gas
And this tried black girl ain't afraid of dying *either*

i
Am already *dead*, iffen I ain't free!
Naw, there is no turning back –
I am saying it loud –
I am black and proud
Just open up the damn door
And I will get it myself!

1983: Groppi Saw Parallels Between New North Division and McDowall School Site
Both built for segregation

1983: Groppi Agreed that Bussing had had Tragic Consequences

Had been pushed by "intellectual types" (no strong mass base of support for it in either black or white community)
Tragic consequences of bussing Unsupervised kids on busses
Black couldn't enjoy their new school (North)
Groppi: "There's a little dehumanization in pushing for "integration"
Doesn't want his own kids bussed, but he wants them to attend integrated schools Specialty status would exclude too many blacks

---

Specialty School: Milwaukee, Wisconsin

Specialty schools —Oh don't worry
We got it under *control*
We'll just close down all the inner city schools
And bus those black kids to the *far* South side

It doesn't matter if they miss 4 hours a day
Of school time
Cause those blacks are *safe* on that yellow bus

Specialty schools —Oh don't worry
Have no fear cause their black teachers will always be near
We will put them in separate room from our white kids
And
When it comes to lunch
Those blacks will eat last and with their own kind

Specialty schools –Oh don't worry
We got it under *control*
By the time they catch on to our
"Segregated" oops – I mean "Specialty" plan
We will have a few inner city schools open

We will fix it up with the best-of – the-best:
Teachers
Equipment
And the latest textbooks
And we will call it a
"Specialty Schools"

That way we can kill two birds with one stone
First, white parents who can't afford to send
    Their kids to "private" schools will have a "*good*" school for
    Their kids
Second, we will limit the number of blacks into our school
From their *own* neighborhoods

Yes. That sounds like a winner: Specialty Schools
Oh don't worry
We got it under *control*.

Groppi on Communal Nature of Life in Freedom House

Groppi: "I see a kind of Christianity there that is unbelievable. One of the guys has a pack of cigarettes, and he walks into this freedom house. It's everybody's pack. A guy has two bits. It's everybody's two bits."

Communal: Nature of the Freedom House

If my brother had a loaf of bread
It was broken in pieces and shared among all
Just like my *brother* did at his *last supper*

If my sister shed tears
Her tears became an embraced wave of sorrow
Melted away like snow under the sun

When one's skin was pierced by a flying stone
It became a punctured wound
Shield by a human band aide
Thus
Each extend hand became a bridge –way
Straightening the crooked path
Foot prints of *ghostly* breeders

Sunday, October 8, 1967: Gregory Used Humor to Defend Black Christmas at St. Boniface Rally
Gregory: "I boycotted Christmas once and saved 8,000. I've been boycotting it ever since."

Black Christmas
(1967)

No jolly white beard
Snowy hair, rosy white cheeks
No oversized crimson suit climbing down
The inner city's chimneys tonight
Singing: *Ho-Ho-Merry Christmas*

No green pine trees adored with
Red
Blue
Green
And yellow lights

No rushing to K-Mart
Target or Toys-R-Us
To buy the Bobbie Doll for TeTee
Or
Little red wagon for Bobby Lee

No Mr. Carrot nose snowman or Rudolph's red nose reindeer(s)
Handing around my door
No flashing glittering signs: Happy Holidays
Nor wrapping paper for hidden gifts

Instead:
A family gathered around the dining room table
Feasting on a good delicious own-home cooked meal:
Juicy fat butterball fried turkey

Pineapple based honey ham
Bay leaf favored Red Kinney beans and rice
Mustard Greens

From my Muddear's back-yard summer garden
Sweet potato cake
Served with fresh homemade lemonade

Surrounded by
Haughty laughter
Over who burned the cornbread

While exchanging handmade gifts
From the heart:
A knitted pink and yellow baby blanket for my
Sister's first newborn
Readings of a written love poem
From the children
To our Muddear and Paw-Paw for their endless love

A Loving Family Shedding tears of joy over
Grand Paw- Paw's whale of a fishing joke
Widely smiling as he reached for a fork
To savor his favorite treats from the table display

At our Black Christmas
There were
No jolly white beard Santa Claus
With snowy hair rosy white cheeks
No oversized crimson suit climbing down
The inner city's chimneys

Just
A loving family and priceless friends gathered together
Under one roof
At one table
And sharing a "down-home" dinner made from heaven.

Father James E. Groppi

Courageous, Wise
Changing, Motivating, Organizing
Memories of fall, 1964
Oak

ME

Assertive, Creative
Building, Seeking, Soaring
Memories of summer, 1967
Niger

REFERENCES

Aukofer, Frank (1968).City with of Chance. Milwaukee
Insults Hurled At Groppi along the March, Milwaukee: The
Bruce Publishing Company, 1968, August 8 p. 112

Aukofer, Frank (1983). Groppi Ambivalent About the Link between
his Italian-American   Background and his Activism.
Interview April 19, 1983; 1989 Auto tape (7) (8).

Aukofer, Frank. (1967) City with a Chance. Groppi Wanted an
Institutional Church Building Milwaukee: Bruce Publishing
Company, 1968; 1982.

Becker, Dismas (1985). Groppi Moralistic, Not PoliticalInterview
by John Derge, March

Becker, Dismas (1987). Groppi Often Maudlin and Depressed
Interview by John Derge, March.

Berry-Butler, Shirley R. (1994) Bertha-Mae, Whoopi and Me
Nzingha Untied (Poetry) Nzingha Publishers Milwaukee,
Wisconsin p. 78.

Cullen, Michael D. (1972). "A Time to Dance: The Michael Cullen Story as Told to Don Ranly" Groppi Frightened by Death Threat Groppi to Cullen. (Celina, Ohio, 1972) July 13, 1970.

Economist (1967) "Priest on the March". Groppi Willing to Die for the Cause Oct. 7, 1967 p. 225

Galesburg (Illinois) (1969). Groppi Admitted That He Was "No Longer Needed" Due to Maturation of the Black Movement in Milwaukee Registered Mailed. January 31, 1969. Section 1, p. 3.

Goodman, Denise (1969) Thursday January 16, 1969: Groppi Spoke at Wittenburg University, Springfield, Ohio (one minute speech) "Groppi Defends Violence, Power." *Journal Herald* (Dayton, Ohio) January 18, 1969 (FBI – 157-8222-A)

Groppi, James E. (1983). Groppi Transferred From St. Veronicas in 1963 Interview with John Derge, April 19, 1983. (19-20). Auto

Groppi, James E. (1971). Factors Affecting Groppi's Decision to Attend Seminary Interview with John Derge, April 19, 1971. Auto tape.

Groppi- Rogza, Peggy (1987). Interview with John Derge , (auto tape) March 1987

Groppi, James E. (1967). Before Kerner Commission in Washington National Advisory Commission Disorders. September 22, 1967. Testify (1523-24).

Groppi, James E. (1983). Groppi's Love for Children Came Through As He Was Driving His Bus in 1983. He would light-up when children boarded the bus. Interview with John Derge. April 19, 1983.

Groppi, James, E. (1983) <u>A Top Prioity for Groppi was Programs to Increase Bus Safety</u>. Interview with John Derge 1983-1984

Groppi, James E. (1983) <u>Groppi Feared Gang Warfare</u> Interview with John Derge April 19, 1983 Auto tape

Groppi, James E. (1983) <u>Groppi: The Northern "Macho Image" Made Violence More Likely in North</u>. Interview with John Derge. April 1983. Auto tape.

Groppi, James (1983) <u>Groppi Saw Parallels Between New North Division and McDowall School Site</u>. Interview with John Derge. April 1983.

Groppi, James (1983) <u>Both built for segregation. Groppi Agreed that Bussing had had Tragic Consequences</u>. Interview with John Derge. April 19, 1983.

Hartnett, Ken (1968) "He's Black, He Suffers What We Suffer." <u>Groppi Felt Blacks Had Right To Lead Their Own Revolution</u>. Miami Sunday Herald May 26, 1976

Hinckle, Warren (1967). "Left Wing Catholics" <u>Typical Scene at St. Boniface During Labor Day Weekend 1967</u> <u>Ramparts</u> 6 November. (21)

Hinckle, Warren (1967) "Left Wing Catholics" <u>Ramparts</u> 6 <u>Summer Day Camp A Crucial Experience for Groppi</u> November 6, 1971.

Hinckle, Warren (1967) "Left Wing Catholics" Nicknames for Groppi – Fall 1967 Groppi's Conception of the Radical Christ Paralleled the Depiction of Christ at *Immaculate Conception Church in Bay View. Ramparts (18) September 15, 1967.*

Hinckle, Warren (1967). "Left Wing Catholics" <u>Groppi on Communal Nature of Life in Freedom House Ramparts 6</u> November 1967 (18).

McGraw, James, R. McGraw (1967) "Swan Song for Nonviolence" <u>Groppi Sat Out 1967 Riots for Pragmatic Reasons</u>. <u>Renewal</u> 7, October 7, 1967. (17).

McGraw, James.R. "Swan Song for Non-violence?" <u>Groppi saw the parallels to Selma.</u> Renewal 7 (October 1967): 15-20.

McGraw, James (1967) "Swan Song for Nonviolence?" <u>Example of Dick Gregory's Humor Fall 1967</u> <u>Renewal</u> 7 October 1967 (15). *Insight* April 25, 1976 (11)

McGraw, James (1967). "Swan Song for Nonviolence?" <u>Groppi Claimed Milwaukee Race Situation as Bad as the South's</u>. Renewal 7, October 7, 1967. (18).

Milwaukee Journal (1967) <u>(Morning) Groppi Vowed Marchers would Continue: Urged Others to Act</u>. September 5, 1967.

Milwaukee Journal (1967)<u>Groppi Spoke to 500 at St. Boniface Rally</u> September 9, 1967.

Milwaukee Journal (1967) <u>Wednesday October 11, 1967 (Day 456) Commandoes led Peaceful March</u>. October 12, 1967.

Milwaukee Journal (1967). <u>Groppi and Marchers Disobeyed Orders Not to March in the Street/Groppi Explained Why</u>. October 10, 1967.

Milwaukee Journal (1967). <u>Groppi and Marchers Disobeyed Orders Not to March in the Street/Groppi Explained Why</u>. October 10, 1967

Milwaukee Journal (1967) <u>Rev Russell Wilton Expressed Desire to</u> <u>"Rehabilitate" Groppi</u>. Friday, September 23, 1967.

Milwaukee Journal (1976) <u>Groppi Advised Children to Demonstrate</u> <u>Instead of Going to School</u>. Monday, September 12, 1967 1:1; 4:1.

Milwaukee Journal (1967) <u>Pre-March Rally of September 11, 1967</u> <u>(Rally 6:30 – 9:10 P.M.)</u> September 12, 1967.

Milwaukee Journal (1967). <u>Groppi Warned of Violence if Open</u> <u>Housing Marchers Failed (At Rally before Maslowski</u> <u>March)</u>. September 22, 1967.

Milwaukee Journal (1967) <u>September 4, 1967: St. Boniface like</u> <u>Brown's AME Church in Selma (Labor Day Weekend)</u> September 5, 1967.

Milwaukee Journal (1967) <u>Peale Opposed Groppi,</u> September 15, 1967. (2.2)

Milwaukee Journal (1967) <u>Sunday, October 8, 1967: Gregory Used</u> <u>Humor to Defend Black Christmas at St. Boniface Rally</u>. October 9, 1967

Milwaukee Sentinel (1967) <u>Wednesday August 23, 1967 –Prentice</u> <u>McKinney and Dwight Benning Announced Plans to Picket</u> <u>the South Side</u>. Wednesday, August 24, 1967.

Milwaukee Sentinel (1979) <u>Saw Bus as His Church</u>. November 5, 1985.

Murphy, Mary Beth (1967) <u>Father Groppi Eldred Lesniewski Afraid</u> <u>to Join Groppi on March</u>. *Milwaukee Sentinel.* November 5, 1985.

Murphy, MaryBeth (1985). <u>Groppi Was A Prophet in Opinion of Duwayne Tollivier</u> *Milwaukee Sentinel.* November 5, 1985

Murphy, Mary Beth (1985) <u>Ald. Richard Spaulding on Groppi's Continuing Unpopularity</u> *Milwaukee Journal* November 5, 1967

New York Times (1967) Groppi Led Demonstration to City Hall Prior to Council Endorsement of Mayor's March Ban Tuesday, September 5, 1967 p. 37. *Washington Post.* September 6, 1967. (A4). Los Angeles Times – Nicholas C. C

Rocky Mountain News (1973). <u>Groppi Accused U.S. of Racism in Vietnam.</u> June 11, 1973 (8)

Salas-Davis, Barbara (2008) Father Groppi was a Great Religious Leader. Interview with the author. September 20, 2008 at University of Wisconsin-Milwaukee

Tracy, Phil (1971) "Groppi" *Critic* Groppi<u> had Mixed Feelings about St. Veronicas at the End</u>. March' 1971 (18).

Tracy, Phil (1971) "Groppi" *Critic* <u>Groppi, Unlike Most Students At St. Francis, had Great Love for Underprivileged (Summer Camp, ETC</u> p. 18

<u>Groppi Felt Youth Camp was a Seminal Experience (18)</u> Groppi <u>Objected to the Minstrel Show at St Francis</u> (18) <u>Factors Affecting Groppi's Decision to Attend Seminary (17-18)</u>

Tracy, Phil (1971) <u>Groppi Loved High School Groppi offended by Anti-Italian Prejudice of High School</u>

Tracy, Phil (1983) <u>Groppi Ambivalent About the Link between his Italian-American Background and his Activism</u>. Interview April 19, 1983. Auto Tape (17)

Tracy, Phil (1971) "Groppi," Critic, Groppi's Response to Tear-Gassing at St. Boniface March 1971.

Tracy, Phil (1971) "Groppi" Critic, Without Proof, Opponents of Groppi Alleged Sexual Misconduct. March 1971. (16).

Tracy, Phil (1971) "Groppi" Critic 1967 – Father Jerry Weber (Groppi's co-pastor at St Veronia's Wondered What Had Corrupted Groppi. (16) March 1971 Catholic Herald Citizen (Ethel Gintoft) April 19, 1975

Tracy, Phil (1971) "Groppi," Critic, Before Marches, Groppi Exhorted His Marchers to have Courage/to be Willing to Die if Needed Be. March (14).

Waldheim, Peter (1985). Whites Constituted 30% to 40% of All Marches (1967), But They Had Little to Say in Decision-Making Process, Phone Interview with John Derge. November 11, 1985.

Waldheim, Peter (1985) Groppi Admitted That He Was "No Longer Needed" Due to Maturation of the Black Movement in Milwaukee. Telephone interview with John Derge November 17, 1985

Washington Post (1974) Claimed He Did Not Miss Civil Rights Movement January 6, 1974.

Washington Post (1967) Maier Feared Civil War, Defended his Approach, Denounced Marchers. September 15, 1967. A9

Washington Post (1974) Groppi Calmer and More Reflective January 6, 1974.

About the Author
Shirley R. (Berry) Butler-Derge, Ph.D.

Student Programs:

During her career as a teacher, Dr. Shirley R. (Berry) Butler, PhD. developed and implemented several outstanding programs to mold, shape and motivate children (i.e., Umoja – African American Male Support Group, Nzingha's Little Sisters, Students Against Violence Coalition Committee, Gospel Choir, Student Crisis Committee, Peer Mentoring/Tutoring) and the Founder of Nzingha's African American Children Publishing Company & Blackberry Creations

Books/Articles:

Dr. Shirley R. Berry-Butler has written and self-published the following books, **Child Abuse and Neglect Prevention Strategies: (1990), Nzingha Untied (poetry) (1994), Cause and Effect: A Black Celebration (play) (1990), Instilling a Thirst for Knowledge:**

How to Increase the Academic Performance of Afrikan American Males (1994), The Utilization of Different Communication Skills by Female and Male High School Students (2002), Legendary African American Crossword Puzzle # 1 (2002) AARUSI: A Creative Writing Program [Infusing Black English in the Curriculum for African American High Students] (2002), Rites of Passage: A Program for High School African American Males (2009) and 15 articles featured in the Milwaukee Journal-Sentinel and the Milwaukee Community Journal (1989-2002).

Workshops:

Child Abuse and Neglect for Adults and Children, Creative Writing for Children, Dolls Making, Hair Braiding, Tie-Dye, Publishing, African/American Culture, Story Telling, Jewelry Making Natural Healing Tree Properties, Spiritual Reading, African American Abstract Painting and Staff Development.

Awards:

During her career as a teacher, Dr. Shirley R. Berry-Butler has received the awards: 1989, Four Year Fellowship Award from, the University of Wisconsin- Milwaukee, 1992, Most Outstanding Teacher of the Year Award, from Wisconsin Bell/Ameritech; 1993, Most Outstanding High School Teacher of the Year Award, from the Metropolitan Milwaukee Alliance of Black School Educators (MMABSE); 1994, Black Excellence Award for, from the Milwaukee Times and Channel 6.

Education:

Dr. Shirley R. Berry-Butler earned the following degrees: 1974, BA Degree in Education, from the University of Wisconsin-Milwaukee, 1990, MS Degree in Exceptional Education, from the University of Wisconsin-Milwaukee, 1991, M.A. in Administration, from National Louis University, and in 2002, PhD. in Curriculum and Instruction, from the University of Sarasota and the founder and principal of Nzingha Institute of Creative Learning and Living (Grades 9-12) 2004-2007.

Family:

God is my source and I am blessed with Mr. & Mrs. Minnie/ K.C. Butler (parents), 4 sisters (i.e., Doreatha, Carole, Barbara and Glenda) and 2 brothers (i.e., John and Lawrence). One son, Shane Maurice Berry-Wright and daughter-in-law with Cira two grandsons, Gabriel and Maxwell and an angel husband, John M. Derge.

To Order:
    Milwaukee NAACP Youth Council T-Shirts (i.e., Small,
    Large, X Large. and XX Large)
                [Colors: red/yellow/navy blue and white]

Contact Author at:
    Email: nzingh49imani2003@yahoo.com

For information about the events in this book:
hhtp://www.marchonmilwaukee.org/
http://wbhsm.homestead.com/marchonmilwaukee.html